THE GOLDEN AGE OF

AUTOMOTIVE TOYS

1925 TOYS 1941

Ken Hutchison
& Greg Johnson

COLLECTOR BOOKS
A Division of Schroeder Publishing Co., Inc

The current values in this book should be used only as a guide. They are not intended to set prices, which vary from one section of the country to another. Auction prices as well as dealer prices vary greatly and are affected by condition as well as demand. Neither the Authors nor the Publisher assumes responsibility for any losses that might be incurred as a result of consulting this guide.

Searching for a Publisher?

We are always looking for knowledgeable people considered to be experts within their fields. If you feel that there is a real need for a book on your collectible subject and have a large comprehensive collection, contact Collector Books.

On the Cover:
Hubley 1935 Studebaker Roadster

Cover design: Beth Summers
Book design: Sherry Kraus

Additional copies of this book may be ordered from:

COLLECTOR BOOKS
P.O. Box 3009
Paducah, Kentucky 42002-3009

@ $24.95. Add $2.00 for postage and handling.

Copyright: Ken Hutchison & Greg Johnson, 1997.

CONTENTS

DEDICATION

Dedicated
to my mom

To my special toy collecting friends,
Gates Willard & Rex Barrett

To my dear friend, Tom Huff,
for enthusiastically sharing the joy
of my many interests

To Greg Johnson, whose hard work
and inspired talent let me discover
my toys all over again

To Bob Natkin and Bruce Halle
who brought us together
and gave us a head start

And to the thousands of kids
who did not trash their toys
like we did...
for leaving behind a lot of
very nice toys for us to collect.

— *Ken Hutchison*

Ken Hutchison and his Ferrari Testa Rossa, 1996.

Ken Hutchison and his Ferrari Testa Rossa, 1961.

DEDICATION

First of all, thanks Ken
for sharing your knowledge,
enthusiasm, and delightful collection

Thanks to my parents, Ken and Bev,
for their love and support

Thanks Nick and Ben
for putting up with a dad
who rarely conforms to the norms

Thanks to my special friend,
Adolph Schaller,
for his inspiration and artwork

Thanks to my young friends,
David and Dannielle,
for reminding me of the importance of
playing, pretending, and the joys of toys

Most importantly,
thanks Meredith
for being my wife and best friend
And for your love, encouragement, and passion
that have given my life new meaning.

— *Greg Johnson*

Greg Johnson

ABOUT the AUTHOR

I met Ken Hutchison when I was working with Greg and Ken
on the Children's Cars Project some six years ago.

But it was a couple years before I really began to know Ken.
I came to know him by experiencing everything around him.

There's beauty everywhere.

Beauty...and a love of history...
a sense of wonder...
open to feelings of awe.

Ken is a grownup...but hasn't outgrown
a certain childlike joy and excitement.

Our home is not a house. It's a shared adventure,
driven by a passion for the beautiful,
gnawing curiosity, and focused enthusiasm.

Well, that's Ken Hutchison.
Looking at everything around him is looking at him.
Inside him.

He's complex ... but not complicated.
Ready for fun, laughter, and easy going good times.

Oh, he went to college, was a creative director
in a major ad agency, raced a Ferrari, deals in antiques...
a lot of stuff like that. That's *what* Ken Hutchison is.

But this is about *who* he is.

— *Tom Huff*

ABOUT the PHOTOGRAPHER

Little Greg Johnson was 11 that sleepy summer on
his grandparent's farm. He was just playing in the
dust with his toy cars and letting time drift by.
Then he discovered the dark room kit
in the Sears catalog.

It changed his life.

Greg's eye and the camera became one.
And when most of us saw the scenery,
Greg saw lights and shadows.

In fact, when most of us were admiring a
stunning sunset, I've seen Greg facing the other way,
taking his pleasure in the way the glow of
the setting sun washes a brilliance over the dullness of dusk,
making the familiar magically diffferent.

Photography is his profession and his passion.
As his friend, artist Adolph Shallar, sees it,
"Greg's eye is most remarkable.
He's uniquely able to see everything clearly.
All at once, beauty, flaws, light, form.
He's simply the best."

He's a gently unique personality.
Dedicated to family, friends, and his camera.
All taken together, they are his life.

It was fun watching Greg working on this book.
Toy cars, cameras, companions…it had everything.

Greg is one of those special people who sort of
amble into your heart. And what a trip. I enjoy
Greg every day as my friend…and partner in life.

— *Meredith Johnson*

INTRODUCTION

Collecting automotive toys seemed to start as a virus among men whose childhood years occurred during World War II. During those years of crisis, the iron and steel that might have gone into making toys was reserved for building the weapons of war. We all had several Christmases in a row devoid of toys. Birthdays, too. Now and then a kindly neigbor, whose kids had grown up, would pass along a little iron toy to one of us.

Because most of the truly elegant toys were produced just before and during the Great Depression, most middle-class kids had to be content with more mundane examples. Throughout my childhood, I never knew a kid who had a large Arcade Mack Truck. Or a Buick. Or a Reo. In the late '30s, almost every kid in our neighborhood had at least one large International truck, because they were sold at the International Exhibit at the annual Dairy Cattle Congress...a major event those days in Waterloo, Iowa.

The only other big toys I ever saw were inside a circular snow fence at the DX service station. The scrap drive was on, and this whole circle was full of pots and pans, and some of the most wonderful toy cars and trucks I had ever seen.

Rescuing them was out of the question. This was war, after all. Oh, I thought about those toys, all right. Thought about how to scale the fence to get one...

Well, maybe two.

Six toys maximum.

But I was pretty sure the penalty for this kind of treason was at least jail and lifelong disgrace. At most...the firing squad. So my initiation to some of the finer toys was delayed some 30 years. But the instant I saw those toys...back when I was eight or so years old...I became a serious collector.

In the late 1960s, I began spending weekends trooping from antique store to resale shop to flea market searching for toys. The Chicago Hilton Antique Show was good for a toy or two.

Imagine this: There was no literature around. No publications. No information. And as far as I knew, no other collectors. What made this so exciting is that most of the toys I found, I was seeing for the very first time. So each acquisition was also a thrilling discovery.

I remember finding a 1930 International van in a tiny shop when I was heading to Canada on vacation. It was repainted khaki brown, scruffy as could be, but complete. And every night, after a day of fishing, I would sit in the soft light just staring at it. I had never imagined such a wonderful toy. I paid $40.00 for it — way too much. At the time, antique dealers' rule of thumb was $1.00 to $1.50 per inch. No kidding.

Around 1970, collectors began to discover one another. And by visiting other collections, new and more exciting possibilities opened for us. Small shows further revealed the scope of what was out there. Dale Kelley started selling a 4 page mimeographed publication called, *Antique Toy World*.

Among collectors, it was a trade-only environment. So the ambitious collector had to buy virtually everything he or she could find, in order to build a "trading shelf."

It was a very competitive atmosphere. Although a lot of lasting friendships were built at that time, there was also considerable acrimony that grew into bitter feuds. Most of the feuders are gone now...and the collecting fraternity is much more congenial.

Today, the trade-only concept is gone. In fact, a lot of collectors don't know how to make a trade these days. Now one's ability to collect is directly related to his or her ability to pay. And much of the excitement of discovery is gone. It's been years since I've seen an exciting toy for the first time. With all the information available, including our book, of course, there are very few surprises left.

We've tried to include enough surprises to make our book a pleasure for you to read and review.

The toys we are presenting are mostly from my collection. A few have been supplied by other collectors.

Like most books on toys, this is not intended to be a complete survey. Rather, it's a loving look at some deserving toys through the eyes of Greg Johnson, photographer. He had the pleasure of discovery that most of us can no longer have. And it shows in every plate.

For me, I never enjoyed my toys more. I was able to experience each one again — alone — not swallowed up in the complexity of a collection. I hope you share in my pleasure.

— *Ken Hutchison*

ESTIMATED
VALUES DEFINED

We spend a lot of time at toy shows, not buying but learning. Checking prices. Seeing what's out there.

We follow auction results. We pick the brains of trusted friends who attend other shows — and we listen to collectors' gossip.

We carefully compare the auction prices — often elevated values — with show prices. Not just because we buy ... but because we like to know what our stuff is worth.

The price ranges are based on these criteria:

Condition is number 1.

The *low figure* represents good, unbroken condition.

The *high figure* is for mint or near mint toys.

The range is broad because excellent condition demands such a high premium.

TIN PLATE
TOYS of FRANCE

European tin-plate automobiles and trucks have had two golden ages. First, the era from the introduction of the automobile as a realistic means of transportation — to the beginning of the Great War in 1914. During this period, the finest toys were produced in Germany. Marklin, Bing, and Gunthermann were creating Wagnerian machines in the most elaborate detail, delicious colors, and hand-painted trim.

The second golden age began around 1925 and continued to the outbreak of World War II. This time, although Germany still set the pace in quality and intricate lithography, France moved the toy business into a new era... *realism*.

And Citroen led the way.

Citroen

Around 1923, Andre Citroen provided the world with a breakthrough concept. Promotional toys. The famous auto maker established a toy company — as the story goes — because he wished every French child to begin his vocabulary with just three little words: "Mama," "Papa," and "Citroen." Perhaps not necessarily in that order. An advanced marketing idea and still the definitive act of long-range thinking.

Naturally, the toys of Andre Citroen were perfectly scaled replicas. Authentic to the last detail.

Every collector makes his or her own judgements about what toys are most pleasing to the eye. However, writing about toys gives one a forum for inflicting such individual opinions on others. Yet in pronouncing Citroen toys as truly elegant in their fidelity to the originals, I am in very good company.

Unlike other French toy companies, Citroen didn't simplify their designs to reduce costs. Only Citroen produced toys with delightfully subtle compound curves. Take the Citroen door, for example. It curved top to bottom and side to side — making them very difficult to restore. Most other toys had flat doors tabbed into the body, easily detached and lost.

Citroen doors demanded realistic hinges, because the curved doors wouldn't open without them.

The most pleasing Citroens came in 1:10 scale (around 16" long) and 1:15 scale (around 12"). Plus, of course, the majestic 1:7 scale B14 taxi and sedan. The variety of models produced over the years requires a little careful attention to grasp the distinctions. The photographs will be most helpful in simplifying the task. Basically, the list reads: B2, B12, B14, C4, C6, Rosalie, and Traction Avant (the one Citroen we all know and love).

As each new model was introduced, the toy factory tooled up and quickly delivered new models to the dealerships in factory colors and a wide variety of body styles.

Historically speaking, the toys outlived the real cars to an incredible degree. And with the exception of the Traction Avant, the toys were probably far more distinguished than the cars themselves.

Citroen B2 Paris Taxi. All the glitter of Paris after dark. Gleaming black with canework side panels, it suggests a time when a cab was a rather grand way to travel. The sweep of the front fenders, the canework paneling, the overall grace and elan endow this toy with charm and jaunty elegance.
Scale 1:10 (16").
Estimated Value: $5,500.00 to $8,000.00

This B2 Torpedo was almost loved to pieces, but it was the author's first Citroen and deserves something for that. The early B2 radiators featured a wire mesh screen that lent a marvelous sense of realism. Later it was replaced by a piece of printed paper.

Citroen B2 Torpedo. This is the one that started it all. Elegant in it's detail and absolutely faithful to the design of "daddy's" Citroen, the B2 Torpedo was an instant success. Scale 1:10 (15"). Estimated Value: $1,800.00 to $2,500.00

Citroen B2 Delivery Van. A difficult toy to find, the author was delighted to settle for a "repaint." One of very few restorations in the collection. Twin rear doors open out from the center and latch securely when closed. The originals carried advertising on the side panels — "Bas Marny" or "Lion Noir" logos.
Scale 1:10 (15").
Estimated Value: $2,500.00 to $5,500.00

Citroen B2 "Cloverleaf." Full size, the 5CV Citroen was very small. Strictly minimal transportation. But as usual, Andre Citroen had a trump card. He gave his little roadster a sporting high style that buoyed the spirit at first glance.
Scale 1:10 (13").
Estimated Value: $3,000.00

Citroen B14 Torpedo. This is a very handsome toy. A classic period piece out of the mid-1920s. It is the very definition of pre-Depression touring car styling.
Scale 1:10 (16").
Estimated Value: $2,750.00 to $3,500.00

Citroen B14 Sedan. What a piece of work this one is. Quality on a grand scale — 1:7 scale to be precise. It is huge, lavishly detailed, and built with remarkable precision.
Scale 1:7 (21").
Estimated Value: $7,500.00 to $9,500.00

The giant *B14 Sedan* has four opening doors, double paneled to give its interior an upholstered appearance. The celluloid windows slide up and down.

The **B14** is sort of like the maiden aunt we all had. Overall, she seems a bit matronly. But for those who admire quality, her beauty is more than skin deep.

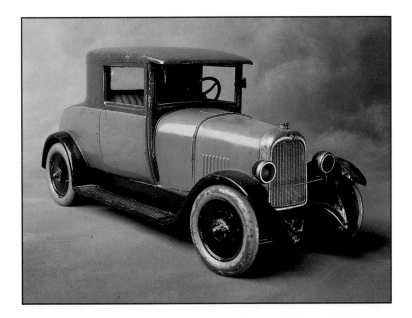

Citroen B14 Coupe. Among Citroen toys, this one is dead common. It is only unique because the body is made of sheet brass rather than steel.
Scale 1:10 (16"). Estimated Value: $1,600.00

Citroen B14 "Farm to Market" Torpedo. It surely looks like the B14 Torpedo at glance. But there's no rear seat, tonneau, or spare wheel. Uniquely, the rear of the body unlatches and folds out, transforming itself into a sort of pickup truck. Here you see it open. Scale 1:10 (16"). Estimated Value: $3,750.00 to $5,000.00

On the ***B14 "Farm to Market" Torpedo,*** when the rear body panel is closed and locked, it fits so well as to be virtually imperceptible. As you can plainly see. Or maybe you can't. This is an extremely rare Citroen model.

Citroen B14 Coupe de Ville. This is a very rare bird. It probably failed to capture the imagination of kids who wanted a toy car just like dad's real one. Since they didn't spend much time being whisked about in town cars, and perhaps weren't dreaming about becoming chauffeurs, it just didn't sell. Sharing the same body as the B2 Paris Taxi, the later B-14 chassis gave it a solid, stolid look. And that took some of the joy out of it.
Scale 1:10 (16").
Estimated Value: $6,500.00+

Citroen B14 and C6 Sedans. What's the difference? That's the whole point behind these photographs. The B14 is in the foreground. When the B14 was superseded by the C6, the bodies were carried over unchanged. But from the windshield forward, fresh and aggressive styling gave the C6 a lighter, livelier look.

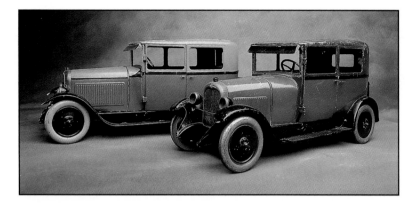

Notice how the taller radiator and hood on the new *C6* (background) permitted the hood to be blended into the body through a fluid cowl design. A color moulding ran from the radiator back through the cowl and along the body. It is surprising how such apparently modest changes so radically perked up the appearance of the C6 compared to the rather dowdy B14 closed cars.

Citroen C6 Sedan. The spectacular colors capture the sensation of a pat of butter floating on Campbell's Cream of Tomato soup. The color alone makes this C6 sedan worth considerably more than a C6 of another color.
Scale 1:10 (16"). Estimated Value: $4,250.00 to $5,000.00

63 Citroen C6 Faux Cabriolet. The looks of a convertible...the snug comfort of a coupe. This style was popular starting around 1928. Even Ford's ubiquitous Model A came in this "false" style. The word "six" on the radiator also identifies it as a C6.
Scale 1:10 (16").
Estimated Value: $2,750.00

Citroen C6 Cabriolets. A trim looking convertible with window frames that stayed up when the top went down, permitting a snug fit and the joy of roll down windows instead of side curtains. In the background, the electric version. The bumpers are the tip off. When the car collided with something, they slipped, tripping the reverse mechanism of the car. Foreground is a clockwork model.
Scale 1:10 (16").
Estimated Value: $3,200.00 to $3,750.00

Tin-Plate Toys of France

Citroen C4 Hire Car. Noteworthy for its unusual seating arrangement, with the folding front and center seats beautifully upholstered in pressed tin-plate steel. This is a C4 (no six on radiator) as are all the 1:10 scale trucks. Apparently it was regarded as part of their commercial vehicles line. Scale 1:10 (16").
Estimated Value: $3,600.00 up

Citroen C4 Oil Tanker. Jaunty and stylish, its eye-appeal lies in its outstanding distribution of mass. At the back, a working spigot lets water flow from the tank. However, there's nothing quite as sorry as one of these put away with water rusting through the bottom of the tank. Scale 1:10 (18").
Estimated Value: $2,250.00 to $3,500.00+

Citroen C4 Fire Engine. One of three variations of the Citroen
fire trucks. Shown with its ladders fully extended.
Scale 1:10 (16"+).
Estimated Value: $2,500.00 to $3,000.00

Citroen C4 Fire Engine. A second style with firemen
and hose reel. It has excellent balance of design.
Scale 1:10 (16" plus reel).
Estimated Value: $2,500.00 to $3,000.00

Citroen C4 Pickup Truck. A very satisfying design, beautifully executed. Note the high hood and tall radiator — common to all C-series Citroens. Another way to distinguish the C-series from all other Citroens is the raised hood moulding that flairs just ahead of the windshield. In the cars, it's painted a contrasting color, but remains body color on the trucks. The exception to the rule is the C4 hire car.
Scale 1:10 (17").
Estimated Value: $2,750.00 to $3,000.00

Citroen C4 Pole and Lumber Truck. Perhaps the superb condition is a tribute to those awkward poles. On the left side, they keep the door from opening and make it impossible to reach the steering wheel. And stuff keeps falling off. It's just no fun to play with.
Scale 1:10 (18").
Estimated Value: $2,300.00 to $3,000.00

Citroen C4 Dump Truck. These were fun to play with. That's probably why I've never seen a really nice one. They were rode hard and put away wet.
Scale 1:10 (18").
Estimated Value: $1800.00

Citroen C4 Faux Delivery Van. It's as faux as faux can be. Phony from the word go. But I had a badly damaged pick up truck and couldn't throw it away. So, salvaged from this junker and built to the author's design by Buddy George, Voila! — a handsome van. The rear door opens. And the craftsmanship is first class.
Scale 1:10 (16").
Estimated Value: no price.

Citroen C4 Hay Truck. This toy came to the author in its original box — assuring that it's not a modified pickup truck. An extremely rare model. And a collector's delight. But for little French kids, a dangerous, frustrating, and uninspiring toy to play with.
Scale 1:10 (20").
Estimated Value: $4,000.00+

Citroen C4 Coupe. The 1:15 scale C-series cars and trucks are all C4s. The louvres do not run all the way to the front of the hood panels — just enough louvres to cool a cheaper 4-cylinder engine. And few enough to let your neighbors know you skimped on your Citroen. This C4 Coupe is very handsome indeed — even prettier than the sedan — usually not the case with C-series Citroens.
Scale 1:15 (12").
Estimated Value: $2,400.00

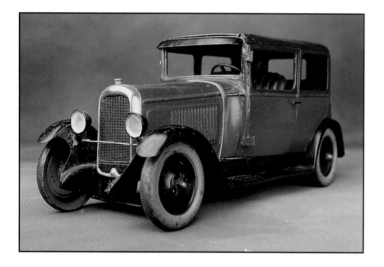

Citroen C4 Petite Sedan. The 1:15 scale Citroens began with a B14 coupe and went on through a series of C4 cars and trucks, and the handsome Rosalies in three delicious flavors. They're all about a foot long and handsomely detailed.
Scale 1:15 (12").
Estimated Value: $1,800.00

Citroen C6 Constructor Chassis. A learning experience. It came neatly packed in a large, flat box. And it's not nearly as much fun to assemble as promised. Many a French father learned to henceforth provide his son with Citroen toys ready built.
Scale 1:10 (16").
Estimated Value: $800.00 to $1,500.00

Citroen C4 Platform Truck. The "Plain Antoinette" of the lineup — it looks like a boring board on a truck chassis. And so it is. But hark...is that thunder rolling black and savage skies our way? "Get out the sandbags and head for the levee, boys!" Having fun with this Citroen is 90% imagination. Get the picture?
Scale 1:10 (17").
Estimated Value: $1,500.00 to $1,800.00

Citroen C4 Semi with Horse Trailer. Like all the 1:15 Citroen C4s, it does not have electric lights. Rather it is fitted with nicely sculptured blanks. The have a sort of Orphan Annie look at times, but are visually appealing. This one is like new. Enjoy.
Scale 1:15 (18").
Estimated Value: $2,500.00

Citroen C4 Street Sweeper. Rare. Rare. Rare. And utterly charming. This one came from the Brian Garfield Jones collection in England. It's near new. And a total delight.
Scale 1:15 (13").
Estimated Value: $3,250.00 and up

Citroen Rosalie Coach/Coupe. During the golden age of classic cars, Andre Citroen found a way to make a mundane two-door sedan into an elegant coach for the middle class. As Huey Long put it, "Every man a king."
Scale 1:15 (12").
Estimated Value: $2,500.00

Citroen Rosalie Roadster. One of the unfortunate results of the Great Depression of the '30s was that so few of the interesting automotive designs of the period were delivered in replica to the toy store. The Citroen Rosalies are a refreshing exception. Their classic 1932–33 styling is elegant — even though the toys themselves were less perfect in their construction than before. This Rosalie Roadster looks just right.
Scale 1:15 (12").
Estimated Value: $2,750.00 to $3,000.00

Citroen Rosalie Brougham. The close coupled look was in, and Citroen wasn't about to be left out. Nice balance. Nice lines.
Scale 1:15 (12").
Estimated Value: $1,800.00 to $2,500.00

Citroen Traction Avant. The car the police used in all those American movies staged in France, the Citroen Traction Avant was a most remarkable car. It was the first commercially successful front-wheel drive car. It remained in production, virtually unchanged, longer than the Model T Ford. And the toy was the most delightful replica toy of the mid-'30s. Not tin plate in the Citroen tradition, the body is one huge aluminum casting — like a frying pan. The fenders and doors are pressed heavy gauge steel. The seats are rubber. And it too is front-wheel drive. It's as different as the car it replicates so well.
Scale 1:10 (16").
Estimated Value: $3,250.00 to $4,000.00

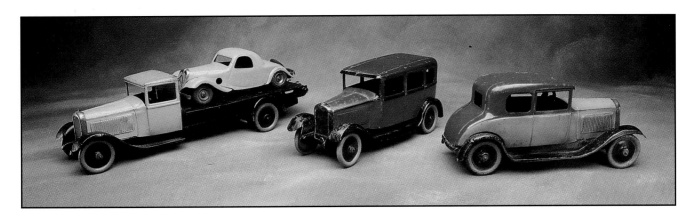

Citroen C6 1:25 scale automobiles. Left to right, C4 platform truck carrying a Traction Avant coupe, C6 sedan, and C6 Victoria coupe. If only they had headlights. Oh, well.
Scale 1:25 (8").
Estimated Value: $300.00 to $600.00

Citroen C4 1:25 scale trucks. Clockwise, milk truck, covered van, stake truck, and dump truck. Platform truck is shown above with cars.
Scale 1:25 (various lengths).
Estimated Value: $350.00 to $900.00

Jouets de Paris

Jouets de Paris produced a series of outstanding toy automobiles in 1:11 and 1:16 scale. To follow Citroen into the world of realism, these lovely cars had readily identifiable hoods and radiators. However, the difference between a Delage and a Renault, for example, ended at the windshield. The bodies, except for color, were identical.

This was even true of their grandest productions — the Phantom I Rolls Royce and the Hispano Suiza dual cowl phaetons — or the Renault and Talbot Lago town cars.

J de P (later to become JEP, by which name it is best known today) automobiles were also late in providing electric lights and opening doors. However the shaft drive drivetrain and forward/reverse transmission was delightfully complex and wonderfully engineered.

So although JEP toys lack the authenticity of Citroen toys, they have a sporting panache that gives them lively eye appeal. Enjoying the joyous elan of JEP sedans, torpedos, and town cars is primarily an emotional experience — supported by an appreciation of their excellent fit and finish.

JEP Delage Limousine series I. These early sedans featured a huge spotlight — a simple, dramatic way to achieve electric lighting. On the side, a large Claxon horn. And on the back, a series of elegant chrome strips to keep the luggage off the paint. And the dramatic fender sweep added a jaunty air to a large sedan.
Scale 1:11 (13").
Estimated Value: $2,400.00

JEP Delage Limousine series II. Time took its toll on the series I cars, and JEP coped with it all by using smaller wheels and putting a trunk on the back. Electric lights replaced the spotlight. The effect was a high topped flop. The Delage fared better than the series II Renault because of long, high Delage hood.
Scale 1:11 (13.5").
Estimated Value: $2,800.00

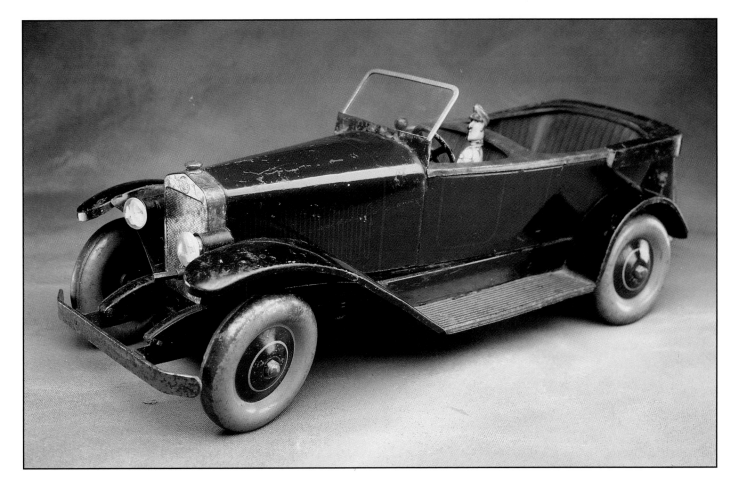

JEP Delage Phaeton series II. Now that's more like it. Without that old-fashioned high roof line, the smaller balloon tires give this phaeton a long, low, sleek appearance. The battery trunk in the back adds to its length, as does the front bumper. This series II JEP Delage really works.
Scale 1:11 (13.5").
Estimated Value: $2,500.00

JEP Delage "Champion of the World" Grand Prix Car. It's right there on the side like a badge of honor — a tribute to French national pride. This JEP is heavy gauge pressed steel, not the traditional tin-plate.
Scale 1:8 (17.5").
Estimated Value: $2,000.00

JEP Delage Grand Prix. While not a precise replica, it is a handsome presentation. The attached remote steering system hardly works. Probably never did, really. The same was used on a Renault 40HP racer. It had a plated grill.

JEP Renault Limousine series II. No magic here. The stopgap modernization effort — smaller balloon tires, bumper, extended trunk — failed to move this Renault into modern times. Baby, the roof's too tall that's all.
Scale 1:11 (13.5").
Estimated Value: $2,750.00

JEP Renault Torpedo series I. Jaunty. That's what it is. That Renault uniquely tapered hood and those swoopy front fenders just work together like magic.
Scale 1:11 (13").
Estimated Value: $2,200.00

JEP Renault Brougham series III. Series III did the trick. These rare close coupled Renaults are very handsome indeed. The balance is almost perfect. The magic is back.
Scale 1:11 (15").
Estimated Value: $3,500.00

JEP 1:16 Renault Coupe series III. The thrifty '30s were upon the world, for the Depression was as wide as it was deep. And the lucky child received one new toy, rather than the usual three or four. No wonder automotive toys of the '30s are relatively rare. Toy companies protected their capital by continuing to produce obsolete models — perhaps updating their details. All this in a decade that saw automotive change go from evolutionary to revolutionary. These little Renaults from JEP were fresh for the '30s.
Scale 1:16 (11.5").
Estimated Value: $1,500.00 to $1,800.00

JEP 1:16 Renault Coupes. Like real cars, these pretty little Renault coupes were available in standard and deluxe trim. The basic difference was the single electric spotlight mounted on the cowl of the deluxe model.

JEP 1:16 Renault Berline. The mate to the little coupes, the Berline style had high fashion beneath a low roof line. Sleek in its close-coupled brougham style, this Renault is Depression cheap (no opening doors, no electric light)...delightful to the eye...and rare.
Scale 1:16 (11.5").
Estimated Value: $2,500.00 to $3,000.00

JEP Renault Town Car. Properly called a cabriolet, this lovely town car was something of a last gasp effort by JEP. This stunning replica of the 40HP "President of the Republic" Renault was an effort to go where the money was and deliver a truly upscale and expensive toy. It failed. But with its spinning fan and clattering valve train beneath its opening hood, it was an aesthetic triumph. Sadly, few of us can own one since so very few were made.
Scale 1:11 (17").
Estimated Value: $6,000.00 to $10,000.00+

JEP Voisin Avions Torpedo series 1. Built by an aircraft designer, Voisin cars were quirky, mechanically and cosmetically. Often wire struts braced the front fenders to the body, aircraft style. JEP Voisins, however, were pretty straight-forward affairs, sharing as they did a common body with more conventional makes. Only the hood and radiator are really Voisinish. All in all, very pleasant looking.
Scale 1:11 (13")
Estimated Value $2,100.00

JEP Delaunay-Belleville and Rochet-Schneider Torpedos series I. The Delaunay-Belleville has a delightful oval radiator and barrel curved hood that give it a strong sense of identity. On the left, the Rochet-Schneider torpedo uses the same body but to a startlingly different effect. The dramatically crisp radiator and hood line do the trick. Even trickier, is the two-tone green lithography divided strangely fore and aft at the cowl.
Scale 1:16 (11").
Estimated Value: $1,250.00 each

JEP Renault Series IV. Renault sedan in the style of the TAV Citroen.
Scale 1:15 (15").
Estimated Value: $1,000.00 to $1,500.00

JEP 1:16 Hotchkiss Limousine series I. In near perfect condition, this little Hotchkiss has one of the prettiest radiators ever put on a toy. These mid-size early JEPs had a simple sidewinder clockwork, but retained articulated steering from the driver's wheel.
Scale 1:16 (11").
Estimated Value: $1,600.00

JEP Voisin Avions Brougham series III. This is one of the "cheap" JEPs. Sidewinder clock-work replaced the elaborate front clockwork powerhouse that drove through a driveshaft to the rear wheels. Non-articulated steering. Stripped down big time. All that having been said, this was a stunner. A low roofline and close coupled body gave it a rakish appearance. Suddenly, the old, old JEP chassis looked like it belonged in the machine age '30s. The Deco days. The ancient clamshell fenders remained, but actually looked racy and glam-ourous for the first time. A new chassis with a '30s fender line soon doomed the last of the original JEP chassis cars. But with this car ... what a beautiful way to go.
Scale 1:11 (13.5").
Estimated Value: $3,500.00

JEP Rolls Royce Phantom I.
The radiator serves to introduce.

JEP Rolls Royce Phantom I. Body, chassis, running gear, details throughout, the Rolls Royce is the twin to the elegant JEP Hispano Suiza. Yet ahead of the windshield, there's the solid, "there'll always be an England" classical hood and radiator. It's all there — the dignity of a government building; the grandeur of an empire.

JEP Rolls Royce Phantom I. Usually painted in cream yellow with raspberry fenders, this particular Rolls is Brewster green with black fenders. It's as subdued as a misty morning on the moors. Sturdy and stately, it hides its sporting style in a somber frock. What a toy. Go ahead...look at it again. Maaarvelous!
Scale 1:10 (19½").
Estimated Value: $8,000.00 to $10,000.00

JEP Hispano Suiza Dual Cowl Phaeton. It swept JEP into the luxury class in high style.

JEP Hispano Suiza Dual Cowl Phaeton. It is surprising that two toys so much the same can be so delightfully different. An elaborate clockwork motor drives this rather massive toy at stately speeds. It sort of chunders along, really.

JEP Hispano Suiza Dual Cowl Phaeton. In this wonderful toy, the divinity is in the details. The claxon horn, delicate windscreens, and daring colors give this toy a dash of — well — dash. The "Spirit of Ecstacy" radiator mascot is obviously out of place on the Hispano. It's classic Rolls Royce. But actually, it appeared on neither toy. Where did it come from? Go figure. Scale 1:10 (19.5").
Estimated Value: $8,000.00 to $12,000.00

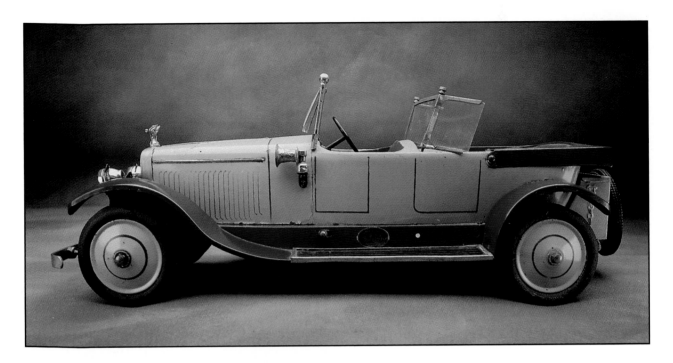

JEP Hispano Suiza Dual Cowl Phaeton. Don't you just love the word "phaeton"? Though it shared the same phaeton body with the Rolls Royce Phantom I, the hood and radiator are unmistakably Hisso. The long springs that gave the Rolls its much ballyhooed ride are not used on the Hispano — though the holes in the chassis are still there.

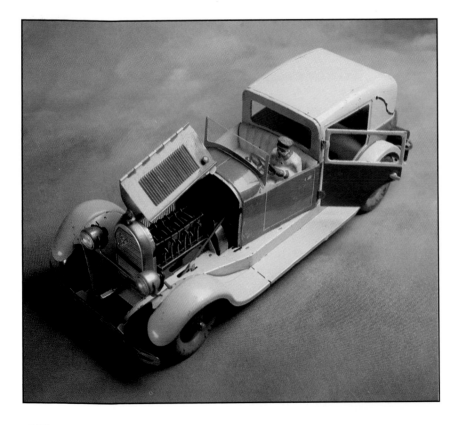

JEP Talbot Lago Cabriolet. From every angle, this is truly a spectacular beauty. Yet it was in reality a sort of cry for help. If Willie Sutton had a good idea (robbing banks because "that's where the money is") then JEP should have hit the jackpot with their elegant, elaborate, expensive Talbot town car. Alas...not so.
Scale 1:11 (17").
Estimated Value: $10,000.00 to $15,000.00

JEP Talbot Lago Cabriolet. This was not designed to please the son of the chauffeur. But rather for the son of the chauffeured. Families who could still afford to settle for the best.

JEP Talbot Lago Cabriolet. JEP was in good company. Going first cabin failed them, but they were hardly alone. Pierce-Arrow, Peerless, Duesenberg, Cord, Franklin — all those who bet on the rich, suffered mightily for it. The great mistakes are greatly prized today. Like this lovely Talbot Lago. Just look at that splendid radiator. Imagine it. All wound up and lumbering along, the engine entertaining with its thrashing valve train and whirring fan blades. Of course, it is at its zenith just sitting quietly. It is art after all.

Charles Rossignol created a line of French toys that spanned half a century or so. My first impression, based on their postwar offerings, was that they were lightweight and flimsy. However, in time I discovered the quality CR toys of the late '20s and early '30s. Even then, some of the parts seemed too fragile to arrive home from the store intact. They are tougher than they look and feel. The survivors tell the tale.

My personal favorites are the Delage Dual Cowl Phaeton, the Renault Town Car, and the Renault bus. Very authentic. One imagines it steaming into Cairo, rods knocking and drive shaft clattering, whopping up its own sandstorm while scattering chickens, pedestrians, cyclists, and other street creatures in its wake.

And slamming to a dusty stop, through the swirling haze, we'd see: disembarking travelers, goats and chickens, and maybe a spy or two.

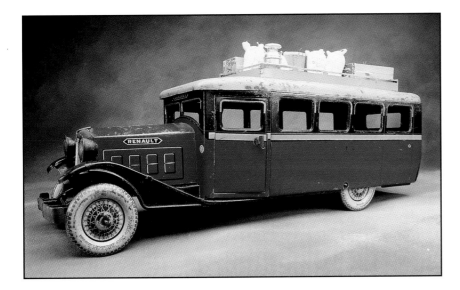

CR Renault Bus. In old black and white movies, one would expect to see such a bus cruising past the Eiffel Tower. But now, it looks more like the last bus to Cairo. It's alive with mystery, intrigue, enigma, and world weariness. It is also a very precise replica of the real thing. It has character big time.
Scale 1:15 (20").
Estimated Value: $3,500.00

CR Delage Dual Cowl Phaeton. Talk about broken dreams...this once proud and elegant toy has fallen on hard times. But perhaps, though originally greatly admired, it lived out its days being much loved. A constant companion of enthusiastically reckless children. Today, it looks like it is best suited for bringing fertilizer bags home ... piled high in the rear seat. Its beauty is sadly dimmed, but little diminished.
Scale: 1:11 (16").
Estimated Value: $1,200.00 to $2,500.00+

How odd that a company known for producing undistinguished (barely collectible) toys, should have created the true masterpiece of the era — the splendid Alfa Romeo P2 Grand Prix Racer. It was so outstanding, it remained in the catalog from 1924 to the invasion in 1939.

Just what was this all about? A racer over 20" long with beautiful wire-like wheels with real knock-off hubs, gobs of real louvres, elegant petrol, oil, and radiator caps, and a stunning wire screen radiator opening. It was — and is — absolutely the finest replica toy ever made. Simple as that.

They did have one more ace up their sleeve over at CIJ. The lovely little 12" Renault Sports Viva. It was a popular toy and remained in the catalogs from around 1933 to 1939. And they sold a lot of them. So a lot of them were roughed up along the way. That's why values vary from $600.00 to $1500.00, because the quality difference is so great.

Alfa Romeo P2 Grand Prix Racer. Sometime around 1924, when a young Enzo Ferrari was making a name for himself racing an Alfa Romeo P2, CIJ introduced this P2, the finest replica toy of all time.

CIJ Alfa Romeo P2 Grand Prix Racer. This is the view many other drivers saw of the real thing. And it looked exactly like this.

CIJ Alfa Romeo P2 Grand Prix Racer. It has everything. Size — a full 21 inches long. And detail. Three beautiful filler caps, beautiful spoked wheels with actual knock-off hubs, leathery hood straps, even Houdaille shock absorbers on the early models, and real louvres ... everywhere!

CIJ Alfa Romeo P2 Grand Prix Racer. Great to the last detail, and that's the delightful screened radiator. The CIJ Alfa enjoyed a long shelf life. Still in the catalogs after some 15 years, it ceased production in 1939 with the advent of war and occupation. Over time, influenced by depression realities, small economies occurred. The Houdaille shocks were dropped, as were the brake drums. But early or late, an Alfa P2 racer is simply fabulous.
Scale 1:7 (21").
Estimated Value: $4,500.00 to $7,500.00

CIJ Renault Sports Viva. If CIJ hadn't produced the astonishing Alfa Romeo P2, this delightful toy would have been enough to earn them a touch of immortality. The Renault Sports Viva seems very American because it so closely resembles the delightful 1933–34 Ford roadsters. It came as a top-up roadster, a cloth-top convertible, a rumble seat version of same, and a spartan model, which lacked both opening doors and bumpers, that came with the Renault Garage. Too bad CIJ didn't have a line of such '30s cars — not so much for children then, but for those of us who are enjoying a second childhood now. Scale: 1:15 (12").
Estimated Value: $650.00 to $1500.00

Small French Cars. Pretty as bonbons, these little delights are pressed steel rather than Tin-Plate. Counterclockwise from center right: CIJ Renault, CIJ Renault 4CV, CIJ Dyna Panhard, Citroen Traction Avant and Rosalie Sedan by Citroen, and a small CIJ Renault. Scale: 1:25 (approx 6")
Estimated Value: $250.00 to $500.00

German
Tin-Plate

In the first decade of the twentieth century, Germany made the finest, most elaborate toys in the world.

Again in the 1930s, German tin-plate toys were among the most excellent toys in design and production ... and were rivaled only by the Japanese in their use of lithography.

Marklin made some very handsome constructional cars and trucks. Gunthermann made a powerhouse limousine with a rollback roof. Hausser built a massive and awesome half track military vehicle. In short, although they weren't as dedicated to realism as the French, or the Japanese, their work was first rate quality and fantastic presentation.

Tippco (TCO) made the most elegant replicas — the foot long Mercedes Autobahn Courier being the most exciting, partly because the real car was such a vibrant beast.

But it was the Fuhrer's Grosser Mercedes, and the companion pieces, that provided the finest detail work. What a pity that Arcade didn't make a cast iron Roosevelt Lincoln for American children — it would be such a treat for collectors today.

Mercedes 800K Fuhrer's car by Tippco. It carried Hitler through parades and into mass ceremonials — so there are pictures of it everywhere. And Tippco (TCO) captured it to the last detail. To admire this elegant toy is not always easy, given the dreadful history of the Third Reich. But taken without the baggage of a sorry past, it is a remarkably precise and attractive toy.
Length: 9".
Estimated Value: $900.00 to $1,400.00

Mercedes trio by Tippco. The staff car and field command car are harder to find than the Fuhrer's car. The sidemount spares disappear on the staff car. And the command car's body is spare indeed. They're all handsomely made.
Length: 9"
Estimated Value: Staff car and Command car, $900.00 to $1,250.00

Maybach Sedan by Tippco. Elegantly swoopy, it carries its mass beautifully. It is especially handsome in profile.
Length: 15½".
Estimated Value: $1,700.00 to $2,500.00

Gunthermann Rollback Transformable Limousine. This is one truly elegant toy. The rollback top has steel side panels which pull up with the top, giving the car the appearance of a closed sedan. Beautifully lithographed.

Length: 18".
Estimated Value: $6,000.00 to $8,500.00,
Record: $12,650.00

Tin-Plate
TOYS of Japan

At the time toy collector's were discovering each other, seeing toys never seen before, and the very first toy gatherings were happening, Japanese toys were generally kept under the table or in a sort of $10 each junk box.

There were two reasons for this:

First, collectors 25 years ago grew up at a time when Made in Japan on a toy condemned it as flimsy and of poor overall quality.

Second, we never got to see the good stuff. The first good one I saw was the 1936 Pontiac Silver Streak. And I swapped $40.00 worth for it.

The Japanese toys shown here are probably the finest replica toys of the 1930s. The lines and proportions are elegant. The lithography is excellent. And the size — one foot or more long — is imposing.

They are extremely rare, and priced accordingly. Since these toys so seldom change hands, price estimates are really guestimates.

12" or longer auto replicas — Very broad estimate: $2,000.00 to $6,000.00+

1935 Chrysler Airflow by CK. Arguably the finest replica of the Airflow ever made, it was issued in solid colors only — with no lithography. Approx. 11".

Two Grahams by CK. The Graham Blue Streak of 1932, designed by Amos Northrup, was the wonder of the year. It's on the left. Its skirted fenders and integrated grill were show stoppers. On the right, an updated model, circa 1935. A different grill and the trunk at the rear are the most obvious changes.
Approx. 12".

1937 Buick, manufacturer unknown. It has the design down, and looks just right.
Approx. 12".

Give it the award for best grill.
Right down to the Buick logo on the right side.

1937 Packard by TN. As elegant as the real thing. Approx. 12".

1932 Packard "Shovelnose" 900 sedan by TN. The Packard logo on the side is a nice touch. Compare it to the 1932 Graham Blue Streak and you can see what made the Graham so advanced. Approx. 11".

1936 Lincoln Zephyr sedan by MT. Not a tin toy, this Lincoln is celluloid. The precision and quality is outstanding. Its survival is a miracle. Approx. 11".

1935 Cadillac sedan by MT. This toy is surprisingly large for a Japanese tin toy. And next to a 12" model, appears to be even bigger than it is. Approx. 15".

1936 Pontiac Eight by CK. Perhaps the most elegant of them all, this Pontiac has the length and distribution of mass one might expect in a 16 cylinder Cadillac. No '36 Pontiac ever looked this good.
Approx. 12".

BRITISH
TOYS at RANDOM

The Brits have made some wonderful toys, mostly 1:43 scale. But there are some larger toys worthy of your notice. We've just selected a few that are interesting and unusual examples. Meccano made very involving constructional toys. The Triang line is made of very handsome 1:25th cars and a lot of trucks. The Sunshine Saloons are the best. The large Triang is quite unusual, however. So here it is. And the Ranlites are wonderfully done. They are something you may not have experienced until now.

Meccano MG/Riley style non-constructional roadster. Hard to find...and so easy to look at. Perhaps the prettiest of the Meccano toys with its classic sweeping British lines.
Length: 8½".
Estimated Value: $800.00 to $1,000.00

Meccano Aston-Martin constructional toys. Meccano made two sizes of constructional cars. Series #1 (shown here) and #2, which were larger and grander. They came with a selection of different parts: tail sections, racing or touring trim, roadster or drophead side panels. You decide. These little Aston-Martin Mark IIs are wonderful replicas. I owned a real Aston-Martin Mark II once. No wonder I like these little ones so much.
Length: 8".
Estimated Value: $600.00 to $900.00

Triang Magic Jaguar SS1 Coupe. To be correct, it's a Swallow SS1. But Mr. Lyons shortly renamed his creation with the more savage moniker...Jaguar. Grrrr. Big and beautiful, this coupe originally had rubber tires over the steel wheels — but I can't find a reproduction tire that fits.
Length: 16"
Estimated Value: $700.00+ (I'm guessing on this one)

Ranlite Austin Saloon. If the Bakelite body has a scratch or dull spot, just sand it with very fine paper, rub it with polishing compound, finish it with a little Simichrome polish, and...Hooray!...it looks like new again. These are heavy, well-built models with a powerful clockwork. And, most interesting, sliding sunshine roof panels. Any collector would prefer that they had headlights, of course. But the overall effect is still extremely pleasing.
Length: 10.5".
Estimated Value: $1,200.00 to $1,600.00

Ranlite Singer Saloon. Distinguishable from the Austin by it side-mount spare tire and elegant front and rear bumpers (the Austin has a luggage rack instead), it's equally handsome. Or more so.
Length: 10½".
Estimated Value: $1,200.00 to $1,600.00

AMERICAN
PRESSED STEEL

This is a huge category. A book in itself. But for this book, we just want to show you four toys...because they're so neat.

So this section is all "show"...and no "tell."

1934 Chrysler Airflow by CorCor. Down in Washington, Indiana, Corcoran Manufacturing was making excellent toys. They didn't make it big in the toy business ... but when it came to toys, they made it *big*. Collectors love the elegant construction and detailing of the Airflows. Especially the beautiful wheel covers.
Length: 17".
Estimated Value: $1,000.00 to $1,500.00

1934 DeSoto Airflow by CorCor. How to tell the DeSoto and Chrysler apart? The DeSoto has a narrower, simpler grill, a single wing hood ornament, and a whole bunch of parallel hood louvres. Length: 17".
Estimated Value: $900.00 to $1,400.00

1932 Graham Blue Streak by CorCor. The styling breakthrough of the year, it was perfect for the folks at Corcoran. And they built it in two delicious flavors. Standard and DeLuxe. The upmarket DeLuxe featured electric headlights, a taillight, and a divided front bumper. They're even bigger than the Airflows. And nothing dresses them up like the chrome wheel discs on some models. Alas, my Graham doesn't have them.
Length: 20".
Est. Value: Plain, $650.00 to $1,000.00
DeLuxe, $800.00 to $1,400.00

1936 Cord 810 by Wyandotte. I personally love the Cord. Love it. And while this toy is not a precise replica, it captures the "look." And the colors and stretched length give it a dazzling Hollywood flash. Wyandotte didn't make many desirable collectible toys…but this is one of them.
Length: 13".
Estimated Value: $350.00 to $600.00

CAST-IRON
CARS & TRUCKS

Cast iron was the material of choice for the Industrial Revolution in this emerging nation of broad shoulders. It's just so *American*.

Railroads led the way ... great iron locomotives running across endless miles of iron rails bringing iron ore to the smelters...and on to the manufacturers...and on to the farms and industries. Sturdy ware for heavy work.

Iron was the foundation on which American enterprise was built.

So while European toy makers must have evolved from clockmakers, American toy companies developed as a parallel activity to basic iron mongering.

Crude as all that sounds, before the turn of the century, cast-iron horse-drawn toys were created with delicacy and style. When it came to cars and trucks, toy producers were very slow to capture the style that would stimulate the imagination.

And it was not until the mid-1920s that cast-iron cars and trucks came into their own — with style and class. Realism burst upon the scene. At the moment cars took on a more unified appearance. So precise replication of the real thing worked like a charm in cast iron. And kids loved it.

And cast-iron toys were well suited to American democratic ideals. By and large, they were available to every family at *blue collar* prices.

No one thought of these toys as "collectible." Their producers couldn't have imagined their products as an art form. They made attractive, sturdy toys that were a good value for the money. Period.

Yet, over the years, cast-iron toys aged with dignity. They "grew" the patina of fine art works. Their baked enamel finishes chipped in a manner that created character.

Cast-iron toys are not an international collectible. They are a slice of American life. An American love affair. True apple pie Americana.

They reawaken in us memories of simple times...where the sunshine was always warm...rain was sweet and gentle...and summertime was endless. A time of honesty, fairness, and generosity. And remind us of the joy of being 7½ years old again.

And they're just so *American*.

Arcade

For those who enjoy automotive replicas, Arcade is your toy store. They were as true to the design as the medium would permit them to be. And the results were toy automobiles, the model and year of which a reasonably astute kid could identify from a couple dozen feet away. Their trucks and tractors were equally precise in their dedication to replicating the real thing.

It wasn't just that they came from a part of the country — Freeport, Illinois — that was reality oriented by nature. Arcade had a better idea, and followed it to its logical conclusion.

They used their dedication to realism as a singular marketing innovation. Before long, International Harvester, Oliver, John Deere, Chrysler, Plymouth, Chevrolet, Pontiac, Buick, Yellow Motor Coach, Checker Cab Company, GMC trucks and buses, Ford, Nash, and more leading companies were selling Arcade products out of their showrooms, and a number of other venues.

At county and state fairs, kids by the thousands ended a day of thrills by riding home in the back seat, sticky with cotton candy, socks ground black with dust, and holding a treasured Arcade John Deere tractor or International truck.

Adults arrived home from "A Century of Progress" in 1933 and 1934 with souvenirs of the World's Fair for the kids. Arcade '33 Fords, Plymouths, those unique GMC World's Fair buses, and 34 Chrysler Airflows.

That was the marketing power of realism. And it provided a strong base for the sale of their toys through more conventional outlets — dime stores, dollar stores, and department stores.

After the war, Arcade failed to return to the toy market in a meaningful way. The entire industry of creating cast-iron toys was over.

Since we are providing price guidance, we should remind the reader that price is reflective of the combination of rarity and beauty of a given design. Unlike some categories of postwar automotive toys that were promoted as "collectible," cast-iron toys toys were created to be played with and are rarely in perfect condition.

Of course, the closer a toy comes to perfection, the higher the price in comparison to lesser examples. That's why, instead of giving precise prices, we are giving a price range that takes into account condition ranging from average to mint.

Sometimes this range is very broad, but that's toy collecting for you.

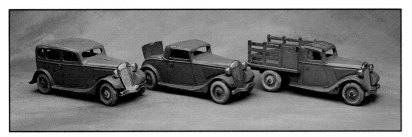

1933 Fords. My favorite is the top-up rumble seat roadster. The entire series is delightful. There's a wrecker that's not pictured because, though I have a few of them, I don't have one that deserves being in this photograph.
Left to right. Fordor Sedan – Length: 6¾".
Estimated Value: $550.00 to $850.00

Top-up Roadster – Length: 6¾". Estimated Value: $900.00 to $1,200.00+
Stake Truck – Length: 6¾". Estimated Value: $500.00 to $750.00+

1933 Plymouths. These Arcade Plymouths are irresistible. I have a dozen or so good ones — and a pile of junkers. In the Taxicab version, the casting is special. The name "Plymouth" was eliminated from the door so a "Yellow Cab" stamp could be applied. These stamps quickly wore off.

Length: 43/4". Estimated Value: Wrecker, $150.00 to $275.00
Taxi, Top-up roadster, Standard Sedan, and Stake Truck, $250.00 to $450.00
Note: condition varies widely among these little toys, because many were very eagerly enjoyed by kids. Others more cherished.

1933 World's Fair Ford Taxi. Well, I was born in 1933. And Chicago celebrated the event with "A Century of Progress." The dashing 1933 Fords were on exhibit. And the lovely Arcade 1933 Ford Taxicabs were on sale. These souvenir Fords were easy to find some 20 years ago. Today...not so. Now they demand a premium price over the less common factory color sedans.
Length: 6¾". Estimated Value: $750.00 to $1,200.00

1935 Pontiac Silver Streak. That's it all right. Perfect!

1933 Pierce Silver Arrow, 1934 DeSoto Airflow, 1935 Pontiac Silver Streak, 1937 Ford V8. The Depression droned on, and the belt-tightening process saw fewer new models introduced. And those few, only in one body style. Sadly, this decade of astonishing advancements in automotive styling had few toys to celebrate the triumphs of "Machine Age" design. Of these, the World's Fair Pierce Silver Arrow is the most unexpected. The Pontiac Silver Streak the most pleasing. The '37 Ford most delightful. And their DeSoto Airflow most unnecessary.

Clockwise from left.
DeSoto Airflow: 6¼". Estimated Value: $350.00 to $700.00
Pierce Silver Arrow: 7". Estimated Value: $300.00 to $700.00
'35 Pontiac Silver Streak: 6". Estimated Value: $350.00 to $700.00
'37 Ford Tudor: 5¼". Estimated Value: $600.00 to $900.00

1934 Nash Brougham. Call it style. And along with the three-window long back coupe (pictured with the group), the little Nash Brougham had it big time. These two cars had an elegance rarely seen in toys of this size. And these toys are rarely seen in any event. They bring serious money because every serious collector wants them.
Length: 4½".
Estimated Value: $350.00 to $600.00

1934 Nash Brougham and Coupe and the truck group. The trucks are often referred to as Chevrolets, even though they used the same grill casting and basic structure as the Nash automobiles. Fair enough, since Nash wasn't a factor in the truck business. The trucks are charming...and much more common than the lovely cars.
Nash Coupe: 4½". Estimated Value: $350 to $600.00
Panel Delivery: 4". Estimated Value: $150 to $225.00
Stake Truck and Wrecker: 4". Estimated Value $85 to $150.00

1935 Ford Sedan. It looks exactly like a 1935 Ford sedan. Easy to love ... hard to find ... it's one of my favorites. And a favorite of every other collector I know. Length: 4½".
Estimated Value $400.00 to $600.00

1935 Ford Sedans and Stake Trucks. One of the stake trucks is repainted. Guess. What a car carrier it would have made with a '35 Ford pulling a load of '35 Ford sedans. Sigh!
'35 Ford trucks: 4½".
Estimated Value $300.00 to $500.00+

Pocket pals: Pontiac, DeSoto Airflow, and Chrysler Airflow. These toys were made to fit into little pockets. Ready to play, any time of the day. So a lot of them are just sort of played out. And as collectors, maybe we should love the much-loved toys the most. But condition is really the end game.
Pontiac: 4". Est. Value: $100.00 to $200.00; Pink or yellow: $175.00 to $300.00
Chrysler Airflow (light blue): 4". Est. Value: $150.00 to $250.00
DeSoto Airflow (red): 4". Est. Value: $80.00 to $135.00

Model A Ford Wreckers. There was a size for every occasion. And price range, too. The one with a bumper isn't quite a Model A — and apparently was sold with other bumper models in toy sets exclusively. At least that's the way I heard it.

Length: 4" (big nickeled wheels).
Estimated Value: $75.00 to $125.00
Length: 4½".
Estimated Value: $75.00 to $135.00
Length: 5½".
Estimated Value: $150.00 to $225.00
Length: 7" (with Weaver crane).
Estimated Value: $500.00 to $750.00

1935 International Delivery Van. My favorite cast-iron truck by far. No contest. This International Panel truck captures mid-'30s design like nothing else. It has grace, elegance, and a charming transitional style. Because of the sweep of the rear end, it is generally referred to as the "Beavertail" International.
Length: 9¼".
Estimated Value: $2,500.00 to $7500.00*

*The value of this toy is enormously affected by condition. At the $2,500.00 value, it may need total restoration. At top dollar, it must be mint original. Mint costs a mint. It is much sought and rarely found.

1935 International Stake Truck. Dramatically long and lean...the very essence of streamline, this creates "The Great Profile." It was too long to be easy to play with, so often survives in quite good condition. The tailgate is sometimes missing, but a replacement is available. The trick is matching the paint.
Length: 11½".
Estimated Value: $2,000.00 to $3,000.00

[front view]

1935 International Dump Truck. This completes the series, but by the nature of dump truck design, it lacks the stunning streamline impact of the other two. I have seen others that were sold with white tires with unpainted centers. Why? Don't know.
Length: 10".
Estimated Value: $1,250.00 to $2,200.00

1930 International Van. The back door opens. The proportions are perfect. The first one I ever saw was a country antique store...in desperate condition. A terrible kid-repaint. Tattered tires. Still, it just blew me away. I paid the $40.00, but it was worth it. I spent most of my vacation evenings just looking at it. Length: 9½".
Estimated Value: Catalog colors $1,500.00 to $2,500.00
Advertising models: $2,000.00 to $4,000.00

1930 International Stake. It looks just right, doesn't it?
Length: 11½".
Estimated Value: $1,250.00 to $2,000.00

White Delivery Van. Style. Character. Charisma. Strength. Power. This truck exudes all this and more. It's the one I want to drive. The White delivery van came with and without sidemount spare tires. With rubber tires or all nickeled iron ones. It's rare and very desirable. The White line included some massive trucks, a bus, and a delightful moving van. And they're all tops.
Length: 8½". Estimated Value: $2,000.00 to "the moon"

1936 *Checker Cab.* The real taxi was manufactured by Checker of Kalamazoo, Michigan. Among toy collectors, however, it is referred to as the "Parmalee" cab, after the East Coast cab company that commonly used this model. A favorite among serious collectors because of its unique styling and handsome proportions. Like all of the more expensive toys of the mid-'30s, it's quite rare. And thus quite pricey.
Length: 8".
Estimated Value: $3,000.00 to $4,500.00+

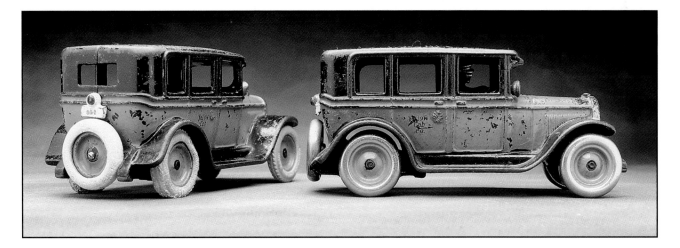

1928 *General Motors Taxi.* It's almost never called that. It's the "Flat Top" cab. Or the "Cowl Light" cab for the nickel over brass headlights mounted on the windshield posts. Note: the windshield posts were often cracked when the lights were installed at Arcade. In my opinion, that's no reason to pass one up. Manufacturer's defects can and should be forgiven.
Length: 8¼".
Estimated Value: Orange, $1,100.00 to $1,800.00
Green, $1,600.00 to $2,500.00
Either color in bank form, add $300.00

1938 International "Cab Over" Stake Truck. International ads called it "a new truck from the ground up." Modern as tomorrow, this replica of a new concept in truck design, was purchased at the International Truck exhibit at the Dairy Cattle Congress in Waterloo, Iowa. I've owned it ever since. I think it cost a dollar back then.
Length: 9½".
Estimated Value: $800.00 to $1200.00

International "Cab Over" Dump Truck. Not nearly as pretty as the stake truck. Much more fun to play with. That's that.
Length: 9".
Estimated Value: $650.00 to $1000.00

1940 International Stake Truck. Less exciting than the elegant 1935 stake truck — and even the 1938 "cab over" — with their separate plated grills. The 1940 model fairly harbingered the end of the line of International trucks by Arcade.
Length: 11½".
Estimated Value: $500.00 to $650.00

1940 International Pickup and Dump Trucks. They completed the 1940 series. And of the three, only the pickup truck really works. It just looks right. And the color helps, too. It makes one wish Arcade had made a 1935 pickup truck, doesn't it?
Pickup Truck: 9¼". Estimated Value: $600.00 to $900.00
Dump Truck: 11". Estimated Value: $500.00 to $750.00

1932 REO Royale. Designed by Amos Northrup, the Reo Royale was a styling milestone at the cutting edge of a 10 year design revolution. Arcade created the flagship of their automotive lineup by replicating this beautiful two-passenger rumble-seat coupe. At the top of their toy line, it was pricey when new. Yet enough of them were made that every serious collector can have one. For a price......
Length: 9".
Estimated Value: (gray or yellow) $5,000.00 to $7,500.00

1932 REO Royales — two for the show. They're just twooo much.

The little REO Royale. Its lines are more graceful ... proportions more pleasing. The separate grill was not plated, but painted to match the body color of the car — just like the real thing. But maybe that's why it was almost the forgotten Arcade toy. A surprising number of collectors seem never to have heard of it. And while they've surely seen one, just never quite noticed it. It is a necessity in any serious collection.
Length: 7½".
Estimated Value: $1200.00 to $2500.00+

Model A Fordor. The large Model A 4-door sedan is not an easy find. Getting this one, with its Kent Motor Co. decal, was a bear. It belonged to a gentleman who did not collect toys. Yet my interest in obtaining it certainly drove up his interest in keeping it. But in the end, two years later, the deal was done. And I guess it was worth it. It is a pretty thing.
Length: 7". Estimated Value: $400.00 to $700.00, W/Decal, $1,500.00+

Arcade Group Shot. These are some of the basics. They provide the foundation for a collection. They are reasonably easy to find and relatively inexpensive. And delight both the serious collector and the beginner.
Clockwise, starting with the black car in the foreground.
Chevrolet Superior top-up Roadster: 6¾". Value: $250.00 to $500.00
Model A Ford Fordor: 7". Value: $400.00 to $700.00
Model A Ford Tudor: 7". Value: $350.00 to $700.00
Model A Ford Stake Truck: 7¼". Value: $300.00 to $550.00

1937 Ford and Covered Wagon Trailer. This is the toy I cut my hair off to get
... by saving the 40 cents I had been given to pay the barber. No wonder I
have two of them. There was a lot of stuff to get over. They were delightful
when I was seven years old — and they still delight me.
Length: 11¾". Estimated Value: $1,000.00 to $1,600.00

Hubley

Hubley was a powerhouse. Lancaster, Pennsylvania, was ideally situated in the most populous part of the country. And their work was excellent. In fact, from time to time they produced a toy so fabulous (and expensive) the first time you see one, it will take your breath away. The mighty Packard Sedan with its opening doors and hood, for example. Or the awesome Elgin Street Sweeper.

While the top of the line was always delightful, their line was complete in the moderate and low price categories. They made Chrysler and DeSoto Airflows from one end of the line to another. Two massive 8" electric light models, three elegant 7½" electric light models, a rakish 6" electric light coupe, and an unlighted 6" sedan. And finally, a little 4" two-door sedan that appears in numbers at every toy show and most antique malls. They're everywhere, those clumsy little rascals. Hubley must have sold a jillion of them.

Hubley had been making toys since the 1890s, but it wasn't until the late 1920s that they began to turn toward automotive realism. Their prime markets were the big cities...and big city kids were surrounded by every make of car. And they could name them all at a glance. Hubley not only gave the kids the realism they yearned for, but they gave them real style trendsetters. The cars of tomorrow delivered today...the dramatically different Chrysler and DeSoto Airflows. The 1935 Studebaker Land Cruiser — exciting fastback sedans — in two sizes. And an array of other body styles for the same chassis. In

1936, it was the ultra streamlined Lincoln Zephyr in three sizes with state of the art house trailers to boot.

And along with avant garde cars and excellent, more traditional trucks, they produced the finest line of motorcycles and airplanes.

Hubley didn't create replica toys with the degree of precise authenticity of Arcade, but in many cases, their colorful complexity was more interesting and involving. Like those cars with a separate chassis which held the body in place with the spare tire. When a kid took a Studebaker apart, the entire headlight-hood louvre assembly fell out. No wonder that today recast units are a popular item.

But it was the electric lights that created the ultimate fascination with the better Hubley toys. They didn't work all that well all the time, but when they did, rolling down the rug at night was a magical motor tour.

As the '30s ran out, the stream of new models ran dry. It was the end of an era. Hubley gave it a good, long run...and did much to make toy collecting the pleasure it is today.

After the war, Hubley motored on, making very fine all metal Ford, Packard, and Duesenberg kits.

The Large 1935 Studebaker Roadster. The Hubley Studebakers, like most of the Hubley entries in the '30s, were not the precise replicas offered by Arcade...but were, perhaps, more reflective of the automotive styling trends of the time. The Studebakers have a strong brand identity combined with pleasing exaggerations of line and proportion. Like many Hubley cars of the time, the spare tire holds the whole thing together. The headlight assembly is often missing, but replacement units are readily available. Condition varied widely from poor to mint — and so do the prices. A kid repaint with broken chassis parts may not be worth purchasing at any price.
Length: 7".
Estimated Value: $250.00 to $550.00

1935 Large Studebakers —
the series. Clockwise from left, land cruiser sedan, town car, dump truck, and roadster. My favorite is the land cruiser for its realism. The town car is by far the most difficult of the cars to find.

Land Cruiser: 7". Estimated Value: $200.00 to $600.00
Town Car: 7". Estimated Value: $250.00 to $700.00
Truck: 7". Estimated Value: $150.00 to $375.00
Roadster: 7". Estimated Value: $250.00 to $550.00

1936 Large Lincoln Zephyr. This was the first American car to have perfectly integrated the streamline principles into a single entity. The Cord 810 was the second. Hubley captured the Zephyr beautifully...right down to the graceful curve that defined the lower edge from end to end. It was Hubley's best replica of the era. Arcade must have been envious. A truly lovely addition to any collection.
Length: 7".
Estimated Value: $350.00 to $750.00

Hubley Lincoln Zephyrs — the series. Hubley so loved the Zephyrs, they made a series of them. The trailer totin" Lincolns pulled an equally streamlined home on wheels, and were actually different in structure from the stand-alone Lincolns. In short, not every Lincoln was capable of pulling a trailer.
'36 Lincoln Large: 7". Estimated Value: $350.00 to $750.00 With trailer: 13½".
With trailer: $500.00 to $1000.00
'36 Lincoln Medium: 6". Estimated Value: $125.00 to $200.00
'38 Lincoln: 5¼". Estimated Value: $75.00 to 125.00
With trailer: 9½". Estimated Value: $250.00 to $400.00

1939 Lincoln Taxi. Far more fantasy than factual design, only the fish fin grills said "Lincoln." Yet it encompassed the generic style of the taxicabs we saw in movies. A few years ago, very expensive. Its value has remained static ever since.

Length: 8".

Estimated Value: $500.00 to $700.00

Its most interesting feature was the flip down luggage rack on the back.

Terraplane Large Coupe, circa 1935. Hubley Terraplanes came in three different sizes. However, the large size has the proportions to make is most appealing. Caution: not everyone calls them Terraplanes, so when buying by mail, a poloroid is almost a necessity. This coupe looks so right. Even the trunkette at the rear which holds on the body looks interesting. This one was the only solid color original I've seen, suggesting it may have been part of a fire fighting set.
Length: 6¼".
Estimated Value: $250.00 to $425.00

Hubley Large Terraplanes — the series. This series of Terraplanes has the only mid-'30s style top-up phaeton I can think of offhand. All things considered, this is a most attractive group of cars. Pictured background to foreground: sedan; phaeton; roadster.
Length: 6¼".
Estimated Value: $250.00 to $400.00; Phaeton add $100.00

Pierce Arrow Estate Wagon. Only Hubley made a station wagon. Their initial offering of the Pierce Arrow series was based on a rather uninspired 4-wheel chassis. This was later upgraded to a much more graceful 6-wheel chassis which included sidemount spares. The bodies for both chasses were identical. Bodies are held in place by a long wire spring that runs from axle to axle, so changing color combinations is very easy to accomplish. Cars and trucks use different chassis designs, with the cars having a trunk. Good to remember when looking for a chassis to complete a car or truck with a body you already own.
Length: 6¼".
Estimated Value: $450.00 to $600.00

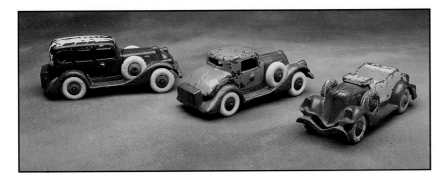

Pierce Arrow Cars. Mix or match colors. Change again and again.
Length: 6¼".
Values: Sedan, Coupe, or Roadster: $325.00 to $500.00

Small Pierce Arrows. At 5" long, the smaller Pierce Arrows have the same elegance of line of the larger ones. Other than the radiator and fender-mounted headlamps, none of them bear particular resemblance to the real 1934 Pierce Arrows. Pictured clockwise: station wagon, roadster, wrecker, coupe, and sedan.
Length: 5". Wrecker: $75.00 to $150.00
Roadster, Coupe, and Sedan: $125.00 to $275.00
Station Wagon: $150.00 to $375.00

1935 Small Studebakers. Lacking some of the grace of the large Studebakers, the smaller ones still offer a lot of style and are extremely pleasing to the eye. One model was not offered in the larger size...and it's a pity. The top-up convertible is very handsome indeed. Length: 5".
Estimated Value, Sedan and Roadster: $150.00 to $275.00
Top-Up Convertible and Town Car: $175.00 to $350.00

1934 Chrysler Airflow Sedan. Majestic toys, the large Hubley Airflows featured electric lights and a wonderful array of interesting nickel-plated detail. They have the heft and feel of real quality.
Length: 8".
Estimated Value: $1,500.00 to $2,500.00

1934 DeSoto Airflow Coupe. Very rare as a toy, as well as in the real cars, the coupe presented a grace of design that gave the airflow concept an airflow appearance. The Airflow Coupe is very difficult to find, and is very pricey.
Length: 8".
Estimated Value: $5,000.00 to $8,000.00+

1934 DeSoto Airflow Coupe.
1934 Chrysler Airflow Sedan.

1934 DeSoto Airflow Coupe. 1934 Chrysler Airflow Sedan.

1935 Chrysler Airflows. Slightly scaled down, more simply assembled than the 1934 models, the '35s had their own style. The roadster and town car especially had a dash of panache. Many of the '35s have chips in the body where it meets the hood ornament. Of the three in the series, the rather understated sedan is the most difficult to find.
Length: 7½".
Estimated Value, Roadster: $1,500.00 to $2,200.00
Town Car: $1,600.00 to $2,500.00
Sedan: $1,800.00 to $2100.00

1935 Chrysler Airflow Town Car. Along with the roadster, it featured a very flamboyant cast aluminum windshield frame. It gives both a slightly cartoony appearance.

1935 Chrysler Airflow Roadster. Like the others in this series, it has electric lights. In the roadster and town car, it is operated by the gearshift handle.

Chrysler Airflows, smaller sizes. Hubley loved Airflows. And they had one to fit any price, and any degree of desired complexity. The smaller sizes include left to right: 4½"; 6¼"; and 6¼". The red fastback coupe featured electric lights yet I have never seen one with the light mounting piece in place and have no idea what it looks like so a replacement might be constructed. Can any of you help out?
Left (common): $75.00 to $125.00
Center: $150.00 to $275.00
Right (rare): $350.00 to $600.00

Power Stack Racer. As it is pushed across the floor, flames appear to fire through the exhaust stacks down the center of the hood.
Length: 10¾".
Estimated Value: $750.00

Mack Telephone Truck. What a nice toy. It looks so right, right down to the water barrel on the side. And it was popular. It came with a pile of accessories, including a really neat pole hole digging auger. They're easy to find...hence the reasonable price.
Length: 9".
Estimated Value: Bell System Green: $500.00 to $700.00
Red: $650.00 to $900.00
With all accessory pieces: add $200.00

Kenton

Kenton, Ohio, was an ideal location for a toy company producing cast-iron toys.

The sheer weight of cast iron made most companies essentially regional because of shipping costs. That's why many of the few toys still coming out of attics are within a few hundred miles of the company that made them.

Kenton could ship east and west, putting New York, Philadelphia, Chicago, St. Louis all within easy reach by rail, and still keep their pricing competitive.

And for most of the first half of the century, Kenton horse drawn toys and later, automotive toys enjoyed a broad market.

Yet, in the East, there was Hubley and in the Midwest, Arcade. Powerful adversaries, both producing very identifiable replicas of real vehicles.

Kenton followed their own star. They preferred to create toys of their own design, borrowing from various realities. The result, generally, were toys of a uniquely jaunty design. Lively. And they exhibited their strength in areas largely ignored by others. Like their delightful calliope and cage circus trucks, backed up by a line of horse drawn circus wagons. And their line of fire trucks and civic vehicles was stylishly designed and quite extensive.

When they did dabble in replicating real automobiles, they were remarkably successful and these models are much sought after today.

Kenton ironwork was exceptional. Their toys were generally thin-cast, stronger than their delicate appearance would suggest. Even their extremely long fire engines somehow survived intact.

Charm, style, dash, sensitive casting, and painting — that's Kenton.

1934 Hupmobile Sedan. "Any way our look at it ... the true air-line car is beautiful" the ad in *Collier's*, May 19, 1934, read. And there's something in what they said. It looks pretty good today. But in 1934, grown-ups rejected the Hupmobile. And so did their kids. So now, there just aren't enough Kenton Hupmobiles to go around. These are very much sought after by even the most advanced collectors.
Length: 7½".
Estimated Value: $2,000.00 to $3,500.00

1934 Hupmobile Sedan and Coupe. In that ad in *Collier's*, it illustrated both sedan and coupe body styles. So the Kenton coupe isn't the fantasy design many have considered it to be. They're interesting, unique, and well executed.
Length: 7½".
Estimated Value: Coupe/Sedan, $2,000.00 to $3,500.00

Circus Cage Truck, large. Only Kenton made the circus come to town with such panache. That jaunty style was so cheerful, they delivered on the promise of good times. Cotton candy, anyone?
Length: 9".
Estimated Value: $1,250.00 to $2,000.00

Kenton Circus Trucks. They came in two delicious flavors, and two sizes to boot. The smaller ones shown here are just as delightful as the big ones ... and maybe a little more charming. They're engagingly cute. Along the way, I saw a third size cage truck — even smaller. But I've never owned one.
Length: 7".
Estimated Value, Cage Truck: $900.00 to $1,200.00
Calliope Truck: $1,200.00 to $1,900.00

Circus Calliope Truck, large. Poop a da poop a da poop! For the benefit of Mister Kite, there will be a show tonight…on Trampoline. And the Kenton calliope sets the tune. And will we still need it when it's sixty-four. Well, yes we do.
Length: 9".
Estimated Value: $2,000.00 to $3,000.00

Willys Knight Sedan. Some toys have something so special, a picture really is worth a thousand words. The Kenton Willys Knight Sedans came in three sizes: a huge 13 incher; a handsome 10" size; and the 8" size shown here. I prefer the appearance of the 8" Willys Knight. It just looks so right.
Length: 8".
Estimated Value: $1,250.00 to $2,500.00+

Pontiac Coupe and Sedan. They came in two sizes, small and smaller. In the large size, a Coupe, sedan, and roadster. They generally came with 1935–1936 Pontiac style grills, but later were recycled with 1938 Chrysler style grills…which seem more appropriate since the bodies look like the '38 roly-poly Chrysler style. They are hard to find. The sedan is possible. The coupe and roadster very unlikely.
Length: 4½".
Estimated Value, Sedan: $250.00 to $350.00; Coupe: $1,000.00 to $1,500.00

Boiler Truck. A powerful looking toy...spectacular with its nickel-plated boiler. It has heft and mass. A great mantle piece.
Length: 14½".
Estimated Value: $900.00 to $1,500.00

The Fire Fighters, *the long, long ladder truck.* No one rivaled Kenton when it came to fire engines and civic vehicles. They made the most...and the most stylish. Most had a plated front bumper that looked so right. This ladder truck is a giant. There's no way to play with it. It's just too long. It can't be turned except on the most slippery surface. I suspect kids tied a string to it and raced it down the sidewalk, its automatic bell ringing.
Length: 22".
Estimated Value: $1,200.00 to $2,000.00

Police Patrol. It's large and handsome.
Length: 9½".
Estimated Value: $450.00 to $700.00

Ice Truck.
Length: 10".
Estimated Value: $750.00 to $1,200.00

Hose Truck. A delightful color. Nice size. Good design.
Estimated Value: $450.00 to $700.00

Wrecker. It came in two sizes, the smaller seems to be rarer.
Length: 9".
Estimated Value: $750.00 to $1500.00

Ladder Trucks. A size for everybody. These two are almost the same size, but not quite. I like the look of the large iron spoked wheels. Ladders are rarely original.
Length: 14" and 12".
Estimated Value: $450.00 to $750.00

Kilgore

Situated quietly in Westerville, Ohio, they were pretty quiet in the toy business, too. They made some wonderful toys, but quality did not progress into quantity.

They made some truly delightful airplanes. And a massive Stutz roadster with some six separate nickel-plated parts, plus a chassis, body, steering wheel and shaft, five wheels and axles. Eighteen parts in all.

But most of their production during the '30s was dedicated to delightful little pocket size toys, many of rather fanciful design.

And though they offered separate body and chassis combinations, their method of keeping the whole works together bordered on the absurd. Apparently all sensible schemes of clipping body and chassis together had been patented, and Kilgore had to re-invent the wheel, which they did by making it square.

To begin with, the axles and wheels were cast in a single iron unit and nickel plated. The rubber tires were fitted to the wheels ... tires that varied from a little too fat to way, way too fat. Because the tires and axles rotated together, the centers of the tires did not wear out as did so many solid rubber tires. Good idea.

Now, here's the really strange part. Hooks on the bottom edge of the body, and bumps on the bottom of the chassis were used to hold an extremely stiff piece of wire in place. Along with holding the chassis and body together, they went under the solid axles to hold the axle, wheel, and tire assembly in place. Whew!

Taking the wire out and putting it back requires tough needle-nose pliers, teeth gritting, and usually a band-aid or two.

They made one series of elegant cars in the '30s. The striking 1932 Graham Blue Streaks. The large size...still just 6½" long...are truly beautiful. Very hard to find. And thus, very expensive for their size. A sedan, coupe, and roadster were offered, my personal favorite being the coupe.

They made a series of smaller size Graham Blue Streaks — coupes, sedans and roadsters. A mere 4" long ... Tootsie Toy Graham size ... they were a pleasure to see and hold. They have very fragile front bumpers so, more often than not, the bumpers were broken off. Threading the wire through the chassis and body of one of these little 4" cars is a serious chore.

Especially in the smaller size, the chassis was painted in a variety of silver finishes, some very tainted with pink or purple hues. Kilgore used some of the most delicate paint colors...their cream yellows and blues being particularly soft and appealing.

Delightful, charming, refreshing, and more than a little eccentric...that's Kilgore.

1932 Graham Blue Streak Coupe. This is the large size Kilgore Graham Coupe. "Large" isn't very ... these cars are only 6½" long. It seems like anything this pretty should have sold by the ton. But these toys are extremely hard to find. Many seasoned collectors are still trying to complete the trio. I prefer the crisp, almost spartan styling of the coupe.
Length: 6½".
Estimated Value: $2000.00+

1932 Graham Blue Streak Sedan and Roadster. These round out the large Graham automobiles by Kilgore. Pretty and petite.
Length each: 6½".
Estimated Value each: $2000.00+

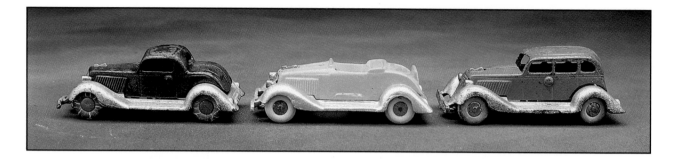

1932 Graham Blue Streaks, pocket size. Tootsie Toy made delightful white metal Grahams the same size. And they sold a jillion of them. Kilgore made them in very high quality cast iron and they're very hard to find. I'm still looking for a nice roadster body. The automobiles are truly beautiful.
Kilgore Grahams, Length: 4".
Estimated Value each: $175.00 to $350.00

The Kilgore wiring system. This is what we were talking about. Those wires are a bear to put in place.

Kilgore Graham Trucks. Ultra-fine castings. Wonderfully delicate grill. Very charming. But none of this is reflected in the price.
Stake, wrecker, and dump trucks: 4".
Value each: $90.00 to $150.00

Pierce Arrow type automobiles. These divide into two groups: three delightful delicate cars: sedan, roadster, and Victoria coupe. These have slender tires and very finely drawn lines. Elegance.
Length: 4".
Estimated Value each: $90.00 to $145.00

The slightly larger coupe and roadster have a wider stance, almost cartoony fat tires, and an attitude. The sheet metal rumble seats are often missing. Not toys you need, but nice to have.
Length: 5".
Estimated Value each: $125.00 to $175.00

A.C. Williams
the clip-on company

Well, this Ravenna, Ohio, company made a lot of toys so crude, they barely qualify as door stops. But they were not without their minor triumphs.

During the '30s, when the take-apart toys gave a kid the option of changing body and chassis color combinations at will, A. C. Williams did it with a vengeance. They'd also sell a single chassis with a sedan body, a coupe body, and a truck body, all neatly packed in a gift box. Of course the catch was this: a kid ended up with one rolling toy. Bummer.

Their method of attaching the body to the chassis was simplicity itself. One short clock spring that clipped into place so tightly it stayed in place, yet was easy to clip on and off. Exceptions to the rule were the 1935 and 1936 Ford sedans, coupes, and roadsters. On those models, the solution was an additional spring steel wire looped through a hole in the top of the grill and extended to the base of the windshield, thus providing a decorative center hood line as well as keeping the grill in place.

Their most impressive entries were a series of 1932 Packards. The largest version of the type 900 "Shovelnose" Packard had beautiful proportions. Even then, they cheaped-out on the headlights by casting them in the fenders. What a splendid toy it would have been had they had sprung for a separate plated grill and headlight assembly.

Aside from a pair of '20s Lincoln touring cars, the Packards, the Fords, and a Chrysler Airflow, it's hard to see why a kid would have chosen A. C. Williams over an Arcade, Kenton, Hubley, Dent, or most anything else for that matter.

They're the kind of toys well-meaning aunts and uncles would buy to disappoint a kid on his birthday. Well, that's the way I see it.

1932 Packard 900 Light Eight Sedan. This was one of A.C. Williams finest hours. They captured the lines of the "Shovelnose" Packard...and the proportions as well. If it had just had a separate nickeled radiator/headlight arrangement, instead of putting the headlights on the fenders Pierce Arrow fashion, they would have created a truely classic toy. This one is quite glorious in blue and red.
Length: 8".
Estimated Value: $550.00 to $900.00

1932 Packard 900s — have it your way. Three color variations: solid blue, blue over red, and solid red. Personally, I would like to find a yellow body that I could put on a red chassis. Wow.

1932 Packard 900 — the lite Light Eight. Just a little bit shorter...an inch, actually ...and yet that's enough to upset the balance and destroy the proportions. They still look great, but not great enough to satisfy the vintage Packard owner. Between the two Packards, a yellow truck on the long 8" chassis.
Length: 7" (truck 8").
Estimated Value: $300.00 to $500.00

A.C. Williams Potpourri. The blue Grahams have charm. The red Reo Sidemount Sedan has style. And the two Plymouths demonstrate the difference between A.C. Williams and Arcade...an exercise which is hardly flattering to the folks at A.C. Williams.
Pictured clockwise from top:
33 Plymouth Coupe, 5¼"; Graham Sedan, 5"; Graham Coupe, 5"; Plymouth Sedan, 5¼"; Reo Sedan, 5".
Estimated Value: Plymouths, $150.00; Others, $120.00

'35 Ford, Dodge Woodie Pickup and Stake Truck. They're hard to find toys, especially the two with separate plated grills. They're cute.
Lengths: Ford Coupe, 4½"; Woodie, 5"; Stake Truck: 4¼".
Values: Ford, $350.00 to $450.00; Woodie, $150.00; Stake, $175.00 to $275.00

Chrysler Airflows. The large one's pretty and nicely done. The small one's cute, but kind of goofy looking.
Lengths: 6½" and 4¾".
Estimated Values: $500.00 to $600.00 and $100.00 to $160.00

A.C. Williams Potpourri. Counterclockwise from bottom right: yellow Packard roadster, Packard coupe, Packard truck, two Rolls Royces, Studebaker truck and coupe, and red Packard sedan.
Lengths: 3½" to 4½".
Estimated Values: $75.00 to $135.00

Champion

Champion it was. A *champion* it wasn't.

Champion Hardware Company, out in Geneva, Ohio, was really in the business of making hardware. During the hard times of the '30s, they turned to toys to keep things going.

Talk about door stops. Champion was the all out champ of crude, with a line of trucks (usually Mack trucks) that didn't reflect toy making as much as indicating iron mongering.

But it seems even the most tedious toy companies manage a moment or two in the sunshine. And their 1934 Dodge coupe was their glittering moment of brilliance.

It was precise, perfectly proportioned, and positively a treat for the most discriminating eye. A kid in our neighborhood — an only child to be sure — had one of these. But he didn't share with anybody. So I only saw the Dodge coupe a couple of times, and never got to hold it. I collected toys for a long, long time before I saw another one. It was damaged, but I was thrilled to get it. A couple of upgrades later, I have a keeper.

There are a couple of other Champions worthy of mention only because they are from Champion: a Reo style coupe and a companion panel delivery, and maybe their Indy style racer.

Times improved and they went back to hardware full time.

And now I've said everything about Champion I can think of, without being truly ungracious.

Champion 1934 Dodge Coupe. Beautiful. Just beautiful.
Length: 7".
Estimated Value: $2,000.00 to $3,500.00

1934 Dodge Coupe.

Potpourri

These toys are a mixed bag. Two were made in Sweden, one isn't even cast iron, and the other two are "manufacturer unknown." What they have in common is that they're uncommonly dramatic and interesting toys of very high quality.

Franklin Victoria Coupe. For years, the only one known was in the Gottschalk collection. Lillian and Bill brought it to the Chicago Toy World Show...so we could all enjoy it. And, I must admit, a good deal of envy crept in as well.

In the past couple of years, two more appeared, dispelling the theory that it was just a prototype.

Lillian called it a *Reo Royale.* But the slope of the grill makes it look like the big *V-12 Franklin* to me. What's your guess? Although someone, somewhere knows who made it, so far that knowledge has not reached the collecting fraternity.

It bears similarities to Dent toys, has some Kenton clues, and seems to me to be from Seto of Sweden. Whoever did it, they created a real beauty.
Length: 10".
Estimated Value: $9,000.00 to $12,000.00

Franklin Victoria.

Franklin Victoria.

Art Deco Roadster. Designed to cut through to the future at 100 miles an hour, this racy roadster has Clark Gable written all over it. Every now and then, a toy designer had a chance to show those Detroit designers a thing or two. And this guy did it. But who made it?
Length: 8½".
Estimated Value: $1,800.00 to $2,300.00

A second look.

1934 Pierce Arrow by Seto. Seto cast two cars that I know of in aluminum. This Pierce and a smaller 1936 Lincoln 2-door. This Pierce Arrow really captures the impact of a large 2-seater coupe — a truly extravagant style. Very elegant.
Length: 11".
Estimated Value: $900.00 to $1,200.00

Bugatti Type 35 by Seto. To start with, I love Type 35 Bugattis. When I saw one pictured in a reprint of the Seto catalog, I had to have one. Easier said than done. It was at least 12 years before I ever saw one. This one. Seto created a masterpiece in a line of cast-iron toys noted for their excellence. It's said that an Arcade employee returned to Sweden and began making Seto toys. Quite believable. His Chevrolet coupe was, well, a copy. But all their other work — precise and charming.
Length: 7½".
Estimated Value: $2,500.00+

NATIONAL PRODUCTS
& other SLUSH MOLDS

The concept of slush molding is so simple as to seem — well — just too easy. Anyone who has worked with ceramics knows the drill. Dump a slurry into a mold. Let it harden from the outside in. Then, at the right moment, dump out the unhardened slurry and Voila! — a perfect, thin-cast piece remains.

Lead soldiers were made this way. Along with some truly lovely automotive toys and replicas. And molding in this manner permitted excellent detail. Our principal interest here is presentation of National Products replicas, although we will show you slush toys from other producers, most under 3" long. Many are very pretty. Some elegant.

National Products of Chicago made the finest examples. These were the first true promotional toys, being distributed through new car dealerships.

The concept was dramatically introduced at the Chicago World's Fair, "A Century of Progress" in 1933. Studebaker's new and rather radical Land Cruiser was a popular souvenir to take home from the fair. Hood louvers updated, it was on the job again for 1934. What made it so appealing was the little assembly line that let the customer order at one end of the line, and then watch their little Studebaker being cast, painted, assembled, boxed, and delivered to them right there at the fair. Pretty neat, huh?

Most of the National Products cars were around 1:28 scale with a few around 1:32. Four large 1:15 scale models were produced. A 1935 Studebaker, '35 and '38 International Vans, and a splendid Diamond T.

Although the general scope of this book is from 1925 to 1941, we're including some of National Products' post war products because all National Products replicas — 1933 through 1950 — are so very collectible.

Studebakers [left to right]: 1933, 1934, 1935, and 1936 models.
Length: 1933–1934, 6". 1935, 6½". 1936, 6¾".
Estimated Value: 1933–34, $200.00 to $300.00
1935, $500.00 to $1,200.00
1936, $500.00 to $1,000.00

1935 Studebaker Land Cruiser. This pretty thing came with its original box. It's perfect. Of all the Studebakers, this 1935 Land Cruiser is the nicest design. It's also quite rare.
Length: 6½".
Estimated Value: $500.00 to $1,200.00

1934 Chrysler Airflow and 1935 Graham Paige. These cars are on a slightly smaller scale than the Studebakers.
Lengths: 5¾" and 5⅞".
Estimated Values: $500.00 to $900.00

1941 Buick Torpedo. It just looks right.

1939, 1940, and 1941 Buicks.
A very handsome trio.
Lengths: 1939, 6⅛"; 1940, 5⅞";
1941, 6⅛".
Estimated Values:
'39 Buick, $500.00 to $1,000.00
'40 Buick, $500.00 to $900.00
'41 Buick, $700.00 to $1,200.00

Large 1935 Studebaker. There were four huge foot-long slush-mold vehicles from National Products. Two International vans, a Diamond T stake truck, and this Studebaker. Awesome.
Length: 12".
Estimated Value: $1,250.00 to $2,500.00

Large 1935 International Delivery Van.
Length: 12".
Estimated Value: $1,200.00 to $2,500.00+

Large 1938 International Delivery Van.
Length: 12".
Estimated Value: $900.00 to $1,500.00

1948, 1949, 1950 Buicks.
Lengths: Approx 6".
Estimated Values: $175.00 to $300.00

1948 Pontiac and Chevrolet Fleetline.
Lengths: 6½" and 6".
Estimated Values: $150.00 to $250.00

1948 Studebaker Starlight Coupe, 1949 Nash Airflyte, 1950 Mercury.
Lengths: 6½".
Estimated Values: $175.00 to $300.00

1948 DeSoto, Dodge, and Chrysler.
Lengths: 6½".
Estimated Value: $150.00 to $250.00

A selection of **Barclays and other small slush molds.** These are tiny pocket toys. Some of them are quite handsome. The more elegant the style, the higher the price.
Lengths: 2" to 5".
Estimated Values: $15.00 to $40.00

WHITE METAL
TOY CARS

For practical purposes, white metal toys and 1:43 scale toys are one and the same thing. True, there are some other scales out there, but 1:43 represents a massive share of what's being collected.

A book could be (and has been) written on this subject. In fact, it would take several books to cover the enormous numbers of toys in this category.

We're just touching on it here because the period 1925–1941 was just the small beginning of an avalanche of such toys. So it's back to the beginning with the two biggies of the '30s. Tootsie Toy and Dinky Toys.

Simultaneously, these two companies, one American and the other British, began creating beautiful automotive replicas — their finest being 1:43 scale. After the war, Dinky Toys resumed production with their pre-war models, slightly modified. We are showing these as examples of their early production.

The most delightful Tootsie Toys are the 1932 Graham Blue Streaks, followed by the magnificent 1934 LaSalles. The Grahams came in a variety of cars and trucks with cars featuring a rear spare wheel, or side-mount spare tires in each front fender or no spare wheel at all. The collector who simply collected Tootsie Toy Grahams in every color and spare wheel variation would have a large collection indeed.

The Tootsie Toy LaSalle came in coupe and sedan form in a wide variety of color combinations. I personally prefer the toy in solid colors, although the silver LaSalle with black fenders in very handsome. The choice of the 1934 LaSalle was inspired. This was a true milestone of design. The trumpet blast announcing the triumphant machine age.

Those Dinky Toys replicas of English luxury cars of the '30s — Rolls Royce, Humber Vogue, Daimler, Bentley to name but a few, — were constructed in the manner of the Tootsie Toy Grahams. Separate plated radiator attached to the body held to the chassis and fender casting by the axles. The result was one of delightful realism.

By the time the '39 series of six American cars come along in 1939, the structure had changed to a one-piece body casting with separate headlights attached where the design required and a pressed steel identification plate on the bottom. I ordered a set of six of these by mail in 1946. This year they will have been in my collection for 50 years.

After the LaSalle, Tootsie Toy never again produced a toy of such delightful quality. Dinky Toys, on the other hand, got the replica message loud and clear. They've been introducing beautiful replicas in a steady stream ever since — with great success.

Note: Values are very contingent on condition. Tops on all of the above would be in the $100.00 range with the exception of the LaSalles which can run to $250.00 or more in mint condition.

Tootsie Toy Graham Paige. One of a vast array of body style and color selections, this elegant town car with its sidemount spare tires is very satisfying.

Tootsie Toy Grahams.

Tootsie Toy LaSalle Coupe. With its narrow grill, streamline circular hood vents, aero style fenders, and airfoil bumpers, the 1934 LaSalle set a new standard in automotive design. LaSalles never again had such a splendid piece of design. Tootsie Toy chose to do this milestone design…and they did it beautifully. For years, the Tootsie Toy LaSalle was the gold standard among international toy collectors. It was Tootsie Toy's finest hour.

Tootsie Toy LaSalle Coupe and Sedan.

Dinky Toys. Clockwise from left: British Salmson 2-seater, British Salmson 4-seater, Rover, Bentley, and Humber.

Dinky Toys Humber Vogue. One of the prettiest of Dinky Toys' body/chassis toys, *Vogue* was the perfect name to describe its classic lines.

Dinky Toys. From left to right: Rolls Royce, Daimler, and Vauxhaul.

Dinky Toys. Clockwise left to right: Buick Viceroy, Studebaker coupe, Oldsmobile coach, Lincoln Zephyr, Chrysler, and the quite grand Packard. This is a favorite series for most collectors.

Dinky Toys. The elegant 39 series Lincoln Zephyr coupe.

AUTOMOBILIA

For car lovers, there's a whole category of collectibles that goes beyond toys. Automobilia. Automotive relics that were created to amuse, enchant, involve, or excite grown-ups. We're including a few examples in this book for that very purpose. Teasers for the adult that's wrapped around our inner child.

So enjoy this visual excursion. We have not included a price guide in this section because such rarities usually change hands after long periods of negotiation — the results of which usually remain very private because the seller is embarrassed at how little he received...and the buyer is embarrassed at how very much he paid.

One example was sold out of the trunk of a car at a tailgate sale for $300.00. A friend of mine offered the new owner $500.00 for it. But he wanted $750.00. No deal. The negotiations continued more or less annually for a dozen years or so. And the offers kept going up...and the price kept going on ahead of the offers. Finally a deal was consummated for around $12,000.00.

There are a couple lessons in this story. First, if you like it a lot and it costs a little more than you want to pay, go for it. It will soon be worth more than you paid for it. Second, while you're waiting for it to appreciate, you will have the pleasure of experiencing it.

1932 Hudson, 1:4 Scale. This is a giant 4-foot long, cast-aluminum model produced by Hudson Motors.

The oral history goes that these were produced for the New York Auto Show. For years, only three were know to exist. A couple years ago, a fourth one was discovered. It needed total restoration. It was advertised for sale at around $35,000.00.

1932 Essex, 1:4 Scale. Essex was sort of Hudson Lite, so it's just slightly shorter. And it's still sitting on the original table used at the New York Auto Show.

Halfway through the year, Hudson dropped the Essex in favor of the all new Essex Terraplane. Hudson had sent the Hudson and Essex models to their leading dealers for display purposes. Well, when the new Essex Terraplane was on its way to dealerships, Hudson told these powerhouse dealers to send the Essex models back to Detroit for destruction. The past was to be the past! One dealer who had a greater appreciation of fine craftsmanship took his Essex home and concealed it in his basement. He told Hudson he had crushed it locally to save shipping costs.

It remained in hiding for some 50 years while a collector wheedled the owner to sell it. Finally, this collector found himself the new owner and headed home with his prize. The story goes that he had put it on the floor of his antique shop overnight. And in the morning, a

couple of doll collectors stopped in. They asked about the Essex. Rather than say it was for display only, he quoted them a very high price — perhaps just to see their jaws drop. They didn't. Instead they began peeling off hundred dollar bills and thwarting his efforts to retreat and save his treasure.

That's how one man owned the collectible of a lifetime, but only for one day. I don't know if this oral history is true but it has the ring of truth to it.

1939 Nash. Apparently these were used in Kenosha by the Nash styling department to help determine paint colors and trim options for the new model year. On one side there are whitewall tires, on the other side, blackwalls. Even the hubcaps are different from side to side. This is a hardwood model neatly finished off with precision metal parts.
Length: 22".

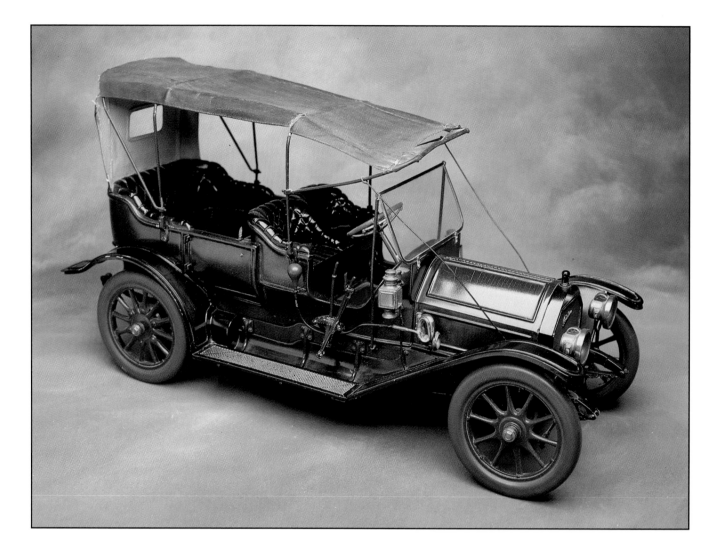

1912 Cadillac. The history of this model is not yet compete. What is clear is that it was built a very long time ago. The top has deteriorated over the decades and paint has crazed along parallel lines which strangely enough are quite attractive. The body is hardwood. The exquisite detailing is brass. It is a very serious piece of work. And an inspiration to behold.
Length: 20".

Frazer-Nash. Not to be confused with the American Frazer or Nash, this was a British sports car known for its chain-drive. This hand-crafted hill-climber was built with a working 4-cylinder engine among a load of interesting details.

Apparently, miniature cars of this type were used by English gentlemen/enthusiasts for miniature hill climb events. How they controlled them is a bit of a mystery to me. The craftsmanship is simply outstanding. The finish — well — rather British. Length: 22½".

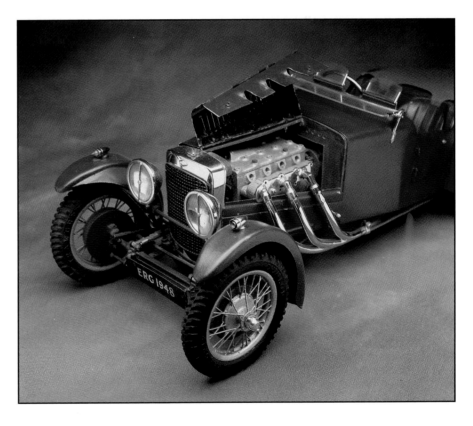

Jaguar XK120 Coupe. One of my all-time favorite cars, this elegant 1:4 scale coupe was a display model. In fact, the rear tires are just half-tires, ending just above the fender skirts. Was it a Jaguar office exhibit? A dealer exhibit? I'd love to know. Much of the original detail was excellent. However, during restoration, we fashioned the kind of window surrounds required to perfect it as a model. We would appreciate any historical information the reader could supply.
Length: 35".

1936 Cord Sculpture. E.L. Cord's famous "Coffin Nose" 810 Cord was introduced at the auto shows as a 1936 model. Things were going badly for that manufacturer of awesome and delightful cars...Auburn, Cord, Duesenberg. 1936 was Auburn's last gasp. Duesenberg was history with a couple of cars being constructed using up the old parts. And the spectacular Cord was brought forth...a bet with everything riding on it.

The Gordon Buerig styling was breathtaking. Plus the car featured front-wheel drive and a pre-selector gearbox. At the auto shows, there was no shortage of buyers who ponied up the down payment and put their names on the waiting list.

But there was many a slip between the show cars and production. Everything was late. And later. And later. And those daring folks who put their money on the line were losing faith and backing out. As a confidence builder, Cord had these beautiful sculptures cast, mounted on peach marble, and delivered to those who were staying the course. Today, they are rare and valuable.

Michele Conti Models The handbuilt models shown here were the artistry of Michele Conti of Turin, Italy. Working with sheet metals from original factory blueprints, he created his models one-off on special order. An admirer of his craftsmanship, I had written several articles about him in the early 1960s.

One day, a package arrived from Michele. A stunning model of the Ferrari Testa Rossa 500 TRC I had raced for a few years. A gift of appreciation from a kind and gentle man. These are a few of his early works.

Later, he produced models in series which were probably more perfectly precise...but these early Conti models had a special sort of character.

Jaguar XK150 Coupe.

Ferrari 500 TRC.

Mercedes 300 SC Coupe.

Aceca Bristol.

Bugatti Type 35.

radiator closeup

CHILDREN'S
AUTOMOBILES

Back in 1968, I opened Volume 6, Number 4 of *Automobile Quarterly*, and discovered a form of automotive magic I knew little about. There before me were a dazzling array of children's automobiles in an article titled, "The Mini-World of Francis Mortarini."

Mortarini had spent years gathering cars built for the most privileged kids in all the world. Bringing these stunning miniature automobiles from throughout Europe and the Middle East to his shops outside Paris, he lovingly restored them to prime condition.

A few years later, the collection was sold and began traveling the world, moving from owner to owner. In 1985, they made their second appearance in the United States, and I contacted their new owner in hopes of making a deal on the C6 Citroen. Instead, we traded full-size Ferrari race cars, and most of the Mortarini children's cars came my way.

In fact, the trucks came, unloaded the cars on my lawn, and were gone. With the help of neighborhood kids, we spent the afternoon moving furniture out of the house...and moving the cars in.

And there I was, surrounded by my favorites from that old Automobile Quarterly article. What a surprising development. And what a pleasure they are. A delight to adults primarily...adults who deep-down feel their parents done 'em wrong. These cars do that to you.

We are grateful to Discount Tire Company of Scottsdale, Arizona, who had these wonderful photographs of the children's autos taken by Greg Johnson for use in their 1990 Progress Report.

1926 Hispano-Suiza Boulogne H6B. This is the one that started it all. It's been called "the world's largest toy," but that doesn't do it justice.

The 1926 Hispano-Suiza Boulogne H6B was discovered under the ruins of a building after World War II, and the first kid's car to be restored by Francis Mortarini. It had originally been created for the Esders family. They are best remembered for their ownership of one of the six Bugatti Royales — a gigantic roadster without headlights as Mr. Esders did not drive after dark. What's overlooked is that a number of Hispano-Suizas enjoyed residence in the Esders' garages.

That's how the very wealthy Esders was able to cajole Hispano into building this awesome tapertail speedster on a 1912 Bebe Peugeot chassis.

It is huge. A full ten feet long. All aluminum coachwork. Marchal headlights (apparently his kid drove after dark). Absolute first class. Classic car quality all the way.

Of all the cars in this collection, it is the most magnificent. And besides, it looks fabulous in the living room.

Hispano-Suiza model H6B. This second Hisso was created by Cattaneo, the noted constructor of racing cars. It features an inlaid burl walnut dash, Zeiss-Ikon headlights, and one of the most beautiful radiators one could imagine. The stork mascots on these Hispanos are said to have taken 120 hours each to fabricate from solid billets of brass. It is some 8 feet long, and alive with louvres. Yet it is the polished aluminum hood that captures the imagination.

Citroen C6 Cabriolet. The largest of the Citroen toys, this electric was introduced to the lineup in 1932, at a cost of 1200 francs. Among its curiosities, it has an ashtray for those sophisticated little smokers of the time. At just over 6 feet, its proportions are perfection. And the coupe de ville top a delightful addition.

Bugatti Type 52. Bugatti actually gave the baby Bugatti an official number. It was, indeed, a replica of the fabulous Type 35, legendary winner of over 1000 races. Bugatti built some 104 of these delightful little electrics, beginning in 1927. They were supplied in two different wheelbases. This short wheelbase model is just over 6 feet long.

Bugatti Replica of the Type 43. A one-off example built by the Bugatti agent in Prague, Czechoslovakia, in 1934, this little gas powered model had it all. A transmission, a center-section rear end, shaft drive, and actual crank starting. It's full of delightful detail. So very Pur Sang. In 1939, it was smuggled out of Prague under enemy fire by a Czech patriot.

Amilcar CGSS. This is everybody's favorite.

Car guys want to "get small" and go bombing around in the little Amilcar. Created by an Amilcar dealer named Martin, it was driven at speed around the race course at Montlhery by a courageous kid, as an advertisement of the brand. The steering is dangerously direct, and with its 125 cc power, it had to be a handful. The chassis is hardwood, coachwork aluminum alloy. The engine and components are alive with polished brass and aluminum. It's 6' 5" long. Mortarini referred to this as one of the most beautiful models in the world...if not the most beautiful.

Maserati Formula I. At least that's the badge that's on it now. Apparently it was at one time regarded as a Gordini, but its got the Maserati lines down cold. A one-off model, it features a front engine, rear drive layout — the power being transmitted through a bizarre system of belts and pulleys. It bears strong resemblance to a 1950s Indy car. It's 7' 3" long.

Cisitalia Formula I. The real car was designed in 1947 by Porsche. A rear-engine car with a 4-cam V-12 putting out 450 horsepower. It didn't ever realize its potential. This model, created by Piero Patria for his son Franco, has a 175 cc motorcycle engine. It's 7' 9" long...and brilliantly constructed.

Lancia Formula I. I loved the 2.5 litre Lancia Grand Prix car the second I saw a picture of it, with its outboard sponson gas tanks, and dramatic louvres. Alberto Ascari, one of the celebrated drivers of the early '50s, drove one of these cars into the bay during the Grand Prix of Monaco. This delightful child's replica was created for Ascari's son. It's a tight fit, for any kid over the age of 5. The craftsmanship is truly elegant.

Innocenti 950 Sport. Everybody loved the Austin-Healey bug-eye Sprite. But not everybody loved the way it looked. So Innocenti put a bare Sprite chassis together with a pretty convertible body by Ghia. This example was built for display on the Innocenti stand at the Turin Automobile Show. The detailing is excellent. To bad it wasn't a Ferrari California. It's an even 7 feet long.

1958 Stanguellini 1100 Sports. Stanguellini never was a very big player. But their little twin-cam cars were quite successful in European racing's small displacement classes. I remember seeing the 1100 Sports race at Road America. It was wonderfully dramatic in its design. I believe the body design was by Bertone. Because they were small, Stanguellini used this child-size car to draw enthusiasts to their stand at Turin and other auto salons. It's 6' 8" long. A precise replica of the original, it's a visual delight, and perhaps amusement, from every angle.

1959 Stanguellini Formula Junior. In this new racing class, Stanguellini was the state-of-the-art. And Formula Junior World's Champion. Their use of the child-size 1100 Sports must have met their hopes and expectations, because in 1962, this child-size Stanguellini Formula Junior began making the rounds of races and automotive exhibitions. It sure captures the real thing — a car that looked just exactly *right*.

Ferraris. In the early '60s, I raced one. And after that, I collected them. I was one of the founders of the Ferrari Club of America. Everything Ferrari...except a tattoo. So I saved the most exciting for last. There they go. *Ferraaaaaaaaaarrrrrrrri!*

Ferrarina 180 Testa Rossa. Made in some numbers in Modena, Italy, this kid's Ferrari was sold through the Ferrari dealer organization. (Actually, then it was the Ferrari dealer disorganization.) The midwest Ferrari distributor brought this home for his kids... and they must have enjoyed it to the hilt. When I got it, it was a total disaster. I took it home hanging out of the trunk of my car — stopping at McCormick Place for the International Auto Show. I had no fear of theft...and I was right. However, for all the destruction, even the fatigued suspension parts had been preserved in a box. It sat in my basement in a pile for 20+ years. After I got the rest of the collection, I had it restored by Restorations Unlimited of Cary, Illinois. And we did everything right. It is painted to resemble the car raced by Gaston Andrey. 6' 8" long. Top speed: 8.5 miles per hour.

1958 Ferrari 250 Testa Rossa "Sebring." When these cars appeared in 1958, everyone was thrilled by their beauty and their look of high drama. In 1960, an Italian industrialist had this car custom built for his son. The proportions are perfect, better than the Ferrarina. The body is aluminum. It has a few dents and scuffs, but that's the way the real ones looked back in those golden days of racing. 6' 8" long.

1962 Ferrari 250 Testa Rossa "Le Mans." For a short time, Ferrari abandoned their trademark oval grill in favor of a twin nostril design. One delicious coupe was built by Bertone. The 1961 Formula I cars — in which Phil Hill won the World's Driving Championship — used the design to great effect. The Testa Rossa was growing old...and this low-body, high back design was the last act. Don't you love the rear view mirror perched on top of the windscreen? 6' 6" long.

See . . . if your folks had *really* loved you . . .

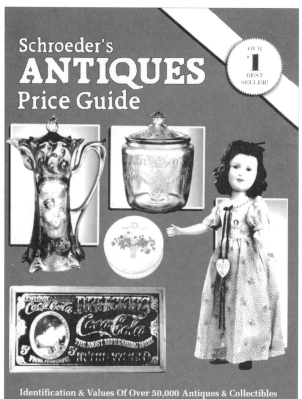